A FOREIGNER's TALE

人88

First published in the United Kingdom in 2017 by Rocket 88, an imprint of Essential Works Limited, 29 Clerkenwell Green, London, EC1R 0DU

Copyright © 2017 Michael L. Jones

The right of Michael L. Jones to be identified as the author of this literary work has been asserted by him in accordance with the Copyright, Designs & Patents Act 1988

Classic Edition ISBN: 9781910978160
Signature Edition ISBN: 9781910978177

Publishers: John Conway & Mal Peachey
Senior Editor: Mal Peachey
Copy Editor: Suzanne Rapcavage
Interviews: Paul Rees
Designer: Barbara Doherty
Cover Illustration: Zara Picken

Printed by Imago in China

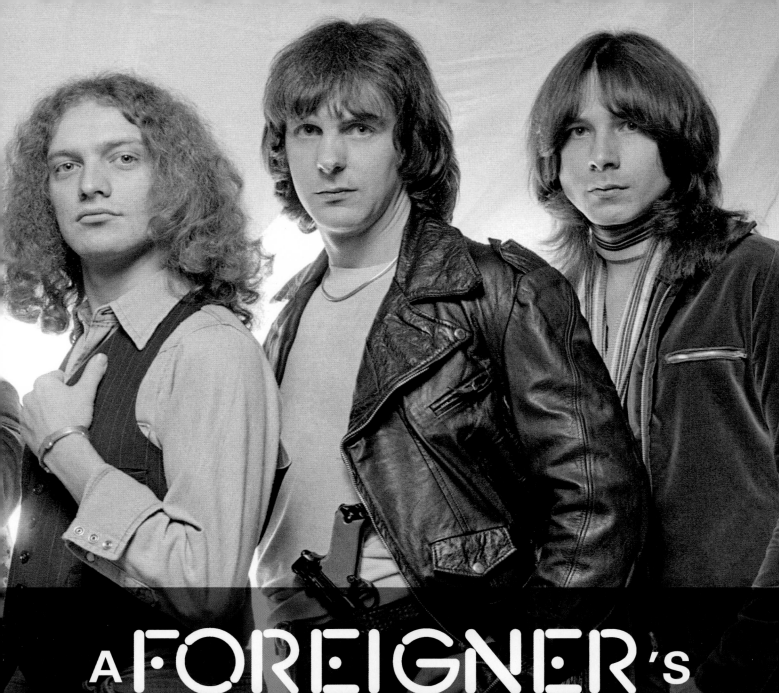

A FOREIGNER's TALE

Mick Jones

I Was Born on the Street

One of my earliest memories is of hearing music in our house. Music first brought my parents together—they met on the dance floor. They both had great taste, were jazz fans and loved to go out dancing, even after they had me. As a four or five-year old I loved being at home with mum as she listened to the hits of the day, and always seemed to be singing along to some record or other on our old radiogram.

Mum and dad were from Portsmouth but they met and were married in Reading, at St. Michael's Church in the suburb of Tilehurst. They didn't have a honeymoon because there was a war on and dad had been conscripted into the army, so was sent off to fight in France following the service. I came along two days after Christmas 1944, and was named after that church in Reading. For a while we lived near London and mum used to tell me how she'd grab me tight and get under the stairs when the "doodlebugs" were flying overhead. She'd be terrified of hearing one of the engines of

Probably taken in 1946; my beautiful mother hugs me for the camera.

HEAD MASTER:
JOHN L. GOODE, M.Sc.

COUNTY GRAMMAR SCHOOL FOR BOYS
WOKING
SURREY

WOKING 1181

TO WHOM IT MAY CONCERN   July, 1962

MICHAEL LESLIE JONES

Michael L. Jones came to this School in September, 1959,
in the middle of his fourth year on transfer from John Ruskin
Grammar School, Croydon.   Naturally, it took some little time
to settle down to this change at such a late stage in his School
career, but he made the transition commendably well.   He
continued to follow the normal Grammar School course leading to
the General Certificate of Education and in this, his second year
in Form V, he sat for the Ordinary Level Examination in English
Language, Geography, French and Mathematics, and his results are
awaited.   In 1961 he was successful in History.

He is not a brilliant boy, but he has worked very well and
I have been pleased with his attitude.   He gained 6th position in
the form last Christmas, and had a high position in most of his
subjects.   I am hoping that he will be rewarded with passes in
the examination subjects he has taken.

He is a boy of sound, firm character, and his behaviour
has been very good.   I believe him to be loyal to his School, he
has shown a co-operative approach to his Form Master, and he gets
on well with his fellows.   In games he has shown himself to possess
special ability.   He is House Swimming Captain, is a member of the
School 2nd Football XI and is also keen on cricket, athletics and
basketball.

He is a boy who, I feel, will develop still further and
give good service to his employers.   I wish him well, and shall
be pleased to answer further questions concerning him.

Head Master

the flying bombs cutting out when it was near, because the next thing you knew it was exploding on or near to you. By the last year of the war though, we were living in Somerton, in rural Somerset, which was to all intents a world away from the action of the war, and the reason why she'd taken me there. Since dad was off in the Royal Marines, mum was the main figure in my life for the first four or five years of my childhood. I was her first and at the time only child, so of course I was spoiled rotten and I can't say that I didn't enjoy the attention. For a good few years after the war as I was growing up, there was rationing but I specifically recall getting little cartons of orange juice and tiny milk bottles from the local shop.

After dad was demobbed, we moved to Woking on the

LEFT: With my dad just after the war.
ABOVE: "He is not a brilliant boy..." a vote of confidence from my old grammar school Head Master. Thankfully, I didn't need to use his reference.

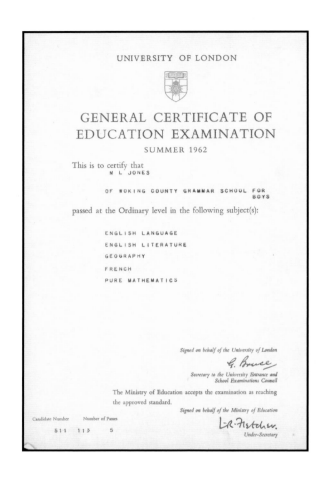

WOKING COUNTY GRAMMAR SCHOOL FOR BOYS

1962 G.C.E. RESULTS: Ordinary Level

Name   M. L. JONES   Candidate's No.   113

Subject	Symbol	Grade
English Language	EN	5
English Literature	EA EB	4
Geography	GY	6
History	H	
Religious Knowledge	RK	
Latin	LA	
French	F	3 oral 3
German	G	
Pure Mathematics	MB	5
Physics	PY	
Chemistry	C	
Physics-with-Chem.	PC	
Biology	BY	
Art	A	
Music	Mu	

Grades   1 - 6   =   Pass
Grades   7 - 9   =   Failure

UNIVERSITY OF LONDON

GENERAL CERTIFICATE OF
EDUCATION EXAMINATION

SUMMER 1962

This is to certify that
M L JONES

OF WOKING COUNTY GRAMMAR SCHOOL FOR
BOYS

passed at the Ordinary level in the following subject(s):

ENGLISH LANGUAGE

ENGLISH LITERATURE

GEOGRAPHY

FRENCH

PURE MATHEMATICS

Signed on behalf of the University of London

G. Bruce

Secretary to the University Entrance and
School Examinations Council

The Ministry of Education accepts the examination as reaching
the approved standard.

Signed on behalf of the Ministry of Education

L.R. Fletcher.
Under-Secretary

Candidate Number   Number of Passes

511   113   5

OPPOSITE: Me aged 10,
at home in the summer
of 1955.
ABOVE: School certificates
of education, awarded to
me in 1962.

outskirts of London. He had a couple of friends who worked in the city and one of them was quite a well-known trombonist, Harry Roche. Dad played the piano and throughout his adult life, I think he secretly hoped to become a professional player, that was his unrealized dream. His great hero was the American jazz pianist Erroll Garner, who had played with Charlie Parker, and in 1955 released the hugely successful *Concert by the Sea* LP, a live recording of his trio performing at the place where the Monterey Festival later began. It had a great cover, with a photo of surf breaking over rocks and a woman in a red jacket with her arms in the air in the foreground. As I recall there's the sound of clapping at the beginning of each side, but it sounds like the sea lapping at the shore, and then the music starts.

1955 NEWLANDS, WOKING

That'll Be the Day

Dad used to let me listen to his records as a child, old 45s and 78s that had a particular smell which is hard to describe, unless you've had a bunch of 1950s-made records in your hands. They were heavy and very deeply grooved black discs of musical delight to me. The first songs that seeped into my subconscious were by Les Paul and his wife Mary Ford, and would have been their hits from the early '50s, recordings of songs like 'Tennessee Waltz' and 'How High the Moon.' They seemed to me to be magical, somehow. I didn't know it then, but Les Paul was an innovator both as a producer and guitarist. He built his own studio in the garage of their house and managed to get all this intricate stuff going on in their records, involving tape echo and reverb. To record his guitar he set himself up in their upstairs bedroom, with leads running down to the garage and somehow created that amazing, distinctive sound. At one point during my childhood, dad got a hold of a whole bunch of bossa nova records, and I was mesmerized by them, too. They must have been all the rage at the dancehall where my parents went dancing, which was probably the Atalanta in Woking, where the floor was famous for being sprung so tightly that it bounced as people danced on it.

My grand moment of musical enlightenment though, came one evening while watching *Sunday Night at the Palladium* on TV with mum and dad. It was the 2nd of March, 1958 and Buddy Holly was a featured guest on the show, which was being presented by Robert Morley. I hadn't seen any singers or guitarists playing live at that point, and no sooner had Buddy walked on stage and started playing 'Oh Boy' than I burst into tears. Mum got up from the

sofa and put her arms round me, she was frantic, asking me if I was OK, but I couldn't even begin to articulate what I was feeling right then. I was completely blown away by this gawky-looking guy with horn-rimmed glasses playing a Fender Stratocaster guitar as he and the two men with him (Joe Mauldin and Jerry Allison) played 'Peggy Sue' and 'That'll Be the Day.' When they finished the audience kept applauding for what seemed like an age, and the curtain never came down, so Morley, a fat man in a dinner suit, had to walk out in front of the band and quieten everyone down. That was the moment that I first knew what I wanted to do with my life, and apparently, I wasn't the only one who was so impressed that night, either. Both John Lennon and Paul McCartney said that seeing Buddy Holly on that show changed their lives. For John it was because Buddy was the first rock 'n' roller he'd seen who could sing and really play guitar at the same time. 'That'll Be the Day' was the first song ever recorded by John and Paul as it happens,

Out of school uniform at last, aged 16.

when they were still called the Quarrymen, just four months after the Palladium show, in July 1958. Eric Clapton wrote something similar in his autobiography, about how as he watched Buddy Holly that night he saw the future of his own life.

You can imagine how I felt when I finally got to play the Palladium myself with Foreigner in June, 2016. Being there that night took me right back to that special point in my life. The curtain worked for us, though.

Being a kid in Britain who loved music in the late 1950s wasn't exactly a golden time. *Sunday Night at the Palladium* was, for a long time, about the only opportunity you got to actually see rock 'n'

OPPOSITE: Les Paul and
Mary Ford with a couple of his
specially built guitars.
ABOVE: The moment that
everything changed for me,
Buddy Holly and the Crickets,
live on British television in
1958.

roll being played live, on a stage. In 1957 the BBC
had started to show *Six-Five Special*, presented
by Pete Murray, but the music acts featured on
it were all a bit tame—people like Alma Coogan
and Tommy Steele were as rock 'n' roll as it
got. Six months after Buddy appeared on the
Palladium though, ITV launched *Oh Boy!*, which
was pretty good, even if it did rely on British rock
'n' rollers for guests, mostly. But at that time
Marty Wilde, Billy Fury, and the Vernon Girls
were the only thing worth watching.

The main outlet for discovering music was
the radio, but that was also pretty limited. On
the BBC, there was a Saturday morning live
broadcast (*Saturday Club*, presented by Brian

Hank Marvin (right), the Brit-
ish Buddy Holly, with white
Stratocaster guitar, Cliff
Richard (center) and Bruce
Welch

Mathews) where at least I was able to hear the latest records by Gene Vincent and Eddie Cochran. If I played with the dial on the radiogram I could find Radio Luxembourg, which would on occasion play other American rockers. The homegrown, British rock 'n' roll scene was then still pretty crummy though, and dominated by Cliff Richard who was nothing like as exciting in comparison with Elvis, Little Richard, or Buddy Holly.

Cliff's backing band, the Shadows (who'd been the Drifters until the Americans of that name became well-known), did at least make an impression on me, and that was because of their guitarist Hank Marvin who, like Holly, played a Strat. Aside from Marvin, to begin with at least, the only other guitarist I was really aware of was Bert Weedon, who was always on the radio. But gradually I discovered other players, and there were a couple of good musicians knocking around Woking. There was one guitarist in particular, a guy named Colin Green, who soon enough became my idol, even though he was only a few years older than I was. Whenever a rock 'n' roll singer came over from the States to play shows in the UK back then, they wouldn't bring their own musicians with them because the musicians union in the UK didn't approve of it, so the stars would have to work with British musicians. They'd usually play as the house band for a roster of Americans on country-wide tours, most of which were promoted by Mr Larry "Parnes, Shillings and Pence," as he was commonly referred to by people who worked for him. Colin would often as not get the gig as the guitarist in what was known as the "pick-up band," which was how he got to play with Gene Vincent, Eddie Cochran, Little Richard, and Chuck Berry before he was 21 years old. It was also how he got to be such a good player. Those tours would commonly involve two performances on one day in a different town every day for a month or more.

Three Steps to Heaven

I became a familiar face to Colin since I was at pretty much every show he played in Woking, whether with a local band or backing a star performer. It wasn't long before we became friends and Colin began to take me with him when he went up to London to play gigs, usually on a Saturday. When he did, early on the day of the gig a few of us from Woking would meet up on the corner of Edgware Road and Marble Arch and do a bit of window shopping and looking in record shops or trying to get into the Two I's coffee bar on Old Compton Street. At first I went along just to get a look at all the American stars who seemed to me like beings from another planet. I was dumb-struck seeing Gene Vincent get off the coach (closely followed by promoter Larry Parnes, I think) that first time Colin asked me along. He introduced me to Vincent and I couldn't think what to say. The funny thing was, I didn't even get to see them play that night, because I was a young teenager and under orders to be home in time for tea. I did get to see Vincent and Cochran on the same bill, at the Finsbury Park Empire in April 1960 though, and they became the backbone of my musical tastes. Mainly because even though I had fixated on the guitar, it was never simply in its own right. From

the beginning I was captivated by hearing it in the context of a band, and with a lead singer.

My trips to London were curtailed when I got a Saturday job, working in a record shop in Woking. That was a gateway to a whole new world of music for me, because the owner used to import records directly from America. I got to handle and hear all the same blues and R&B discs that the guys in the Beatles and the Stones were also listening to (although I didn't know it then, of course). Things like the early Chess Records sides by Muddy Waters, Howlin' Wolf, Bo Diddley, and others. A few years later, when I got to hang out with the Beatles in Paris, they turned me on to Marvin Gaye and Solomon Burke before either American had hits in Britain, but who they'd picked up on already.

A few streets away from the record shop, there was another branch of the store that sold musical instruments. They didn't have a great selection, but typical of the kinds of things you'd see in the British music shops of the late-1950s: there were a couple of acoustic guitars, a steel guitar and maybe a snare drum. It was enough, though, to captivate me. That was where I got

With my first guitar, a
Framus (just like Paul
McCartney had), 1960.

my first guitar—mum took me along one day not long after I'd seen Buddy Holly on TV and bought me a nylon-stringed Framus acoustic (coincidentally the same make that Paul McCartney started out on). I was not much more than 13 and the Framus had a fretboard that was wider than my hand. For the first couple of years of playing I went through agonies trying to bridge those huge spaces until someone turned me on to a smaller neck and steel strings.

I was 15 or 16 before I got my first electric, a Gibson SG that dad signed for on hire purchase. I'm self-taught, because although to begin with at least I took some formal guitar lessons, that was under protest and I was impatient to learn. I wanted to get on with being able to

play songs and so I picked things up by ear, and by using trial and error, which was how a good percentage of the guitarists who came up during that period learned. No-one particularly got around to figuring out how to read music— although they'd all read Bert Weedon's *Learn to Play in a Day* book, apparently. My friend Colin Green was the exception to the rule, since he was more of a classically trained musician. I suppose that sort of formal background might have opened me up to a wider range of music, but in my case I'm not sure that would have been a good thing. Having limited options meant that what I was grasping for was always within my reach—which is the case even today, when I'm writing songs on the piano.

My musical taste was still being set though, and I knew there was still a lot I didn't know, and still hadn't heard. Then one weekend a few of us took a jaunt up to the West End for a party at an acquaintance's house. It was there that I first heard Ray Charles' recording of 'What'd I Say.' I was instantly transfixed and after the record had played through, I picked it up off the turntable and studied it. The most prominent thing about it was its red and black label, on which were written the words "Atlantic Records." That was truly a moment of discovery for me. I thought to myself, "Wow, if this guy is making records for that record label then it must be cool." And from then on, Atlantic Records would remain the standard against which I measured everything.

OPPOSITE: My friend Colin Green, far right, and band-mates (L-R) Red Reece (drums), Clive Powell (aka Georgie Fame) Piano, Billy McVeigh (aka Ray McVay) Sax, Vince Cooze (Bass), with Gene Vincent at Abbey Road studios, 1960. ABOVE: The late, great Bert Weedon, guitar teacher to a generation of British rock greats.

Guitar Boogie

At that time, in the very early 1960s, the area of Surrey I lived in was especially rich in guitar playing talent. Jimmy Page grew up just down the road from me in Epsom. Eric Clapton hailed from but five miles away in Ripley, and Jeff Beck was born a little farther on towards London, in Wallington. It wasn't until several years later that I found out about that proximity; no one then was much interested in where you came from. I once saw Clapton and Beck together in a guitar shop on London's Denmark Street, Lew Davies' I believe it was called (it must have been around 1969). The door opened and the pair of them walked in off the street. They had each ordered a Danelectro double cutaway guitar and had come in to check them out. They sat down on a couple of amps and started jamming away on blues stuff, and I was in heaven.

My first band was called the Hustlers, and was made up of a group of lads from Woking. We used to play pretty much every week at a little clubhouse in the Kingfield area of town and got to be quite popular. Our singer, a guy named Terry Crow, had mastered all of the early Roy Orbison singles, like 'Only the Lonely,' 'Crying,' and 'Running Scared,' but very little else, so by default they were the bedrock of our set. We also got to play the somewhat more prestigious Atalanta Ballroom. By this time the old former Wesleyan Sunday school hall where my mum and

"To Mum and Dad, Thanks for making me what I am, love…"

dad had done the foxtrot and bossa nova
had been turned into a "nightclub," and
for some reason had fish painted along
the walls. On occasion, we would manage
to get a gig as the opening act there
for guys like Gene Vincent or Jerry Lee
Lewis. That was how I got my education,
watching and learning from those kinds
of performers, trying to figure out what
and how they were playing and taking a
mental note of their stage presence.

I was 16, 17 by then and absorbing
all these different influences and
experiences, desperate to make a career

OPPOSITE: Carter-Lewis and the Southerners, featuring the young Jimmy Page, 3rd from left, 1963.
ABOVE: Jeff Beck and Vox stack amps, deafening a couple of admirers, 1966.

out of playing music. It seemed a pretty far-fetched aim, since there were only a couple of British guitar bands back then who were making any kind of money, and that was the Tornadoes (who also toured as Billy Fury's backing band) and Brian Poole and the Tremeloes—both bands were constantly touring, although neither released anything until 1962. I couldn't see how I was even going to get to that level of being a regular gigging guitarist, but I knew that I didn't want to do a nine-to-five job, going up to London and back to Woking every day of the week.

1962 - TALK OF THE TOWN - LONDON

Enter

An act of fate led to me getting my first full-time
gig. One of my old school-friends in Woking,
Roger Mingaye, was playing guitar professionally
in a band called Mike Berry and the Outlaws,
having previously played with Screaming Lord
Sutch. One day, struck down with flu, Roger
called me up and asked if I could sit in for
him for a show in Cardiff. Billy Fury was top of
the bill and Johnny Kidd and the Pirates were
also appearing. The drive to Cardiff alone was
memorable. All that day, I was halfway between
being excited and terrified, but I made it through
the show well enough, and ended the night as a
proper, paid musician.

I was still rehearsing with the Hustlers but we

were not going to become a professional band, and so when I was asked to join a group called Hogsnort Rupert and his Good Good Band, of all things, I said yes. The original Hogsnort Rupert was an art student named Bob McGrath, and his Good Good Band were a rhythm and blues outfit formed at Kingston College of Art with fellow student John Renbourn on guitar (he later became a much renowned folk performer), the wittily named Grapefruit Goodchild on piano, and Dick "Fancy" Forcey on drums. Unusually for the time they had a tenor saxophonist too, Peter (Greg) McGregor.

This was early in 1963 and I'd been to see the Rolling Stones play at Studio 51, which was a basement club two flights down in Great Newport Street. The club had rugs on the floor, and no stage, so they set up in the corner. We were crammed in there, and I was an arms-length away from Mick Jagger, Keith Richards and Brian Jones. There was an incredible atmosphere, the music was loud, and we kind of knew that something special was happening. When I was thinking about this book I was sorting out a bunch of old bill posters that I've kept from that time, and there was one that

Rolling Stones Mick Jagger, Charlie Watts, and Keith Richards performing at Studio 51, a basement club in central London, 1963.

showed that I was on the same bill as the Stones at the Wooden Bridge pub in Guildford in March, 1963. (I didn't get to perform on the same stage as the Stones again until 1989, when I guested with them at their induction into the Rock & Roll Hall of Fame.)

Hogsnort Rupert had drawn the poster himself, and the gig was promoted by the soon-to-be-famous Ricky-Tick blues club, for whom Rupert had created a logo, of sorts. (The original Ricky-Tick in Windsor became famous when a recreation of it was featured in the movie *Blow Up*, with the Yardbirds performing on the stage.) Being in the Good Good band for a short time led to my getting a gig with Zoot Money. Our drummer had played with Zoot and fixed me up with his Big Roll Band. Zoot was a great performer—kind of England's answer to Jerry Lee Lewis—and was heavily influenced by American soul and R&B music.

Not long after that, I took a call from a couple of guys in another working band, Nero and the Gladiators, asking me to an audition. "Nero" was Mike O'Neill, and at the time the only Gladiator was Tommy Brown, the drummer. They'd

just lost their bass player Boots Slade to Georgie Fame's Blue Flames, and guitarist Joe Moretti to Jet Harris' band. They'd had a couple of minor hits with a brace of instrumental tracks, an old circus tune called 'Entry of the Gladiators,' and their take on a classical piece by Grieg, 'Hall of the Mountain King,' but now they wanted to move towards more of an R&B sound. It was most probably Colin Green who tipped them off to me since he'd done a stint in Nero prior to joining Georgie Fame and his Blue Flames. In fact, Nero had something of a reputation for having great guitarists pass through their ranks. Joe Moretti, a Scot, was a really influential player and he had followed Colin into the Gladiators. The two men met on the ill-fated Gene Vincent and Eddie Cochran tour of 1960, when Colin was due to back Cochran the night he had the fatal car crash, and Moretti was backing Gene Vincent. Moretti had played the signature 12-bar riff on Vince Taylor's 1959 'Brand New Cadillac,' which had a huge impact on all of us budding guitarists of the time—you can hear Taylor shout "play it Scotty" just before the guitar break in the middle; he didn't know Joe's name, only that he was Scottish. Moretti

also came up with the intro riff on Johnny Kidd
and the Pirates' 'Shakin' All Over.' So I had to
pack my Vox AC30, which I'd had customized
by Pepe in Denmark Street (that man was a
legend among us guitarists) and follow two
great British rock guitarists into the band, and
play their parts (Colin played on 'Enter the
Gladiators' and Moretti recorded 'In the Hall of
the Mountain King'). That was, if I managed to
pass the audition—which I did, luckily. I joined
Nero and the Gladiators in the winter of 1963
just before I turned 19, and so became part of
a proper touring and recording act (a young
guitarist named Andy Summers took my place in
Zoot's band). Nero had great contacts in Italy—it
was where they'd come up with the name while
touring there in 1960—and had European tours
booked for the next few months. They hired a guy

OPPOSITE: London was in
the grip of freezing fog in
the winter of 1963.
LEFT: Great Scottish
guitarist Joe Moretti, early
1960s.

named Jim Cannon as bassist and we began to rehearse as often as everyone could make it.

I began to really look forward to the idea of foreign travel, because it was bloody cold that winter. At the time I joined Nero I'd just begun work as a trainee estate agent at an office in Mayfair though, and London was suffering some of the last of the famous smogs which froze the soles of my shoes, and made my wool coat heavy with water and coal dust as I tried not to bump into people who'd suddenly loom up in front of me. I couldn't see farther than the end of my guitar case at times. One night that winter, some mates and I were driving back to Woking from London when the fog came down so fast and so densely, that we had to pull the van off the road. The headlights only made things

worse, you couldn't see anything except two brighter bits of fog. We sat in that freezing van for five hours, waiting for it to lift. We couldn't do anything else, certainly not hitch a ride with anyone else, because there weren't many cars daring to drive in that fog.

My working week was made a lot happier by the two nights a week when I changed my usual schlep back to Woking from London and stayed on the train for an extra couple of stops to get to band rehearsals. I had no intention of selling houses for a career, but I'd agreed with my parents to try it out for six months. Obviously they hoped I'd end up forgetting about playing music for a living, and settle down to a more "normal" life. As it happened, I didn't stick it out in Mayfair for more than three or four weeks

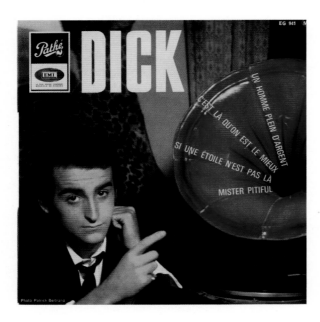

and by October 1963 I had given up going into the estate agents' and concentrated on playing music, learning Colin and Joe's licks. Mind you, I had managed to attend a rather posh dinner at the Talk of the Town that the estate agents had organized before giving it up.

My parents were not thrilled, but things were made easier by Nero and the Gladiators agreeing to play a month-long engagement in France, backing up a French rock 'n' roll singer named Dick Rivers. I needed no encouragement whatsoever to pack my bags and be off. Rivers was fairly typical of what was going on in French pop music at the time. Their hit parade was pretty generic and dominated by French-language versions of better-known English or American songs. Elvis, Chuck Berry, Little Richard, they were the foundation of what was going on, but the French artists would put a chic spin on things—I suppose that was almost a national characteristic. Rivers was an Elvis fanatic and had even lifted his stage name from that of the character Presley played in his second film *Loving You*, Deke Rivers. He'd started out as

the singer for a band called Les Chats Sauvage (The Wild Cats), who in 1961 had caused a riot at the Olympia in Paris while appearing with Vince Taylor. Rivers went solo in 1962 and released his debut album (*Je Suis Bien*) in October 1962. By the time the Gladiators began the tour with him he'd had a solo hit with his first solo single 'On a Juste L'age,' so he was getting decent-sized crowds that were usually full of screaming girls.

A Wild Cat

I loved France. I had been on summer holidays to the country with my parents a couple of times, and was enraptured by the way everything looked and smelled. It appeared to me to be so much more vivid and colorful than gray old London. French had been my best subject at school, mainly because of the enticement the French teacher gave his students to do well. If you got your head down in class and finished the set work before the bell, he would let you go up to his desk and choose from a pile of *Paris*

OPPOSITE: In 1966 Dick Rivers released a song we co-wrote, 'Si une étoile n'est pas là.' BELOW: France seemed to have so much more of everything than England back then, especially delicious food.

The lovely Marie-France;
she introduced me to so
much of life in France.

Match magazines that he had collected, and take one back to your desk. I'd thumb through those copies and gawk at all the radiant images of Brigitte Bardot and countless other French beauties. Now here I was at 18, on my first proper tour, the smell of Gitanes cigarettes in the air, and I couldn't have been happier. The first two or three shows went smoothly, too. I felt comfortable being in the band and we were treated well— that is, until I fell head over heels for a gorgeous French girl named Marie-France Plumer, who just so happened to be Dick Rivers' fiancée. She had been a child star in France in the late 1940s and early 1950s (she was always billed as the French Shirley Temple, of course), and was usually known as La Petite Marie-France, or "the cute Marie-France," and not at all inaccurately. Marie-France was 19 when we met, and extremely pretty. My feelings for her were reciprocated, but acting on it was my first goof as a professional musician.

We were traveling around France in an American station wagon during the tour, and on the long drives Marie-France and I hunkered together on the back seat and would subtly, or so we thought, slip down out of sight of those up front. Of course, Dick soon found out what was going on and had me kicked off the tour. The rest of the band couldn't have cared less; they told me it was my own stupid fault and left me stranded somewhere outside of Bordeaux with just my faithful Scottish roadie, whose name sadly escapes me, for company. I had, though, made an arrangement to meet up with Marie-France at her mother's apartment in Nice. However, that meant to get there the roadie and I had to hitch-hike 500 miles across the country, through the Pyrenees and along the French Riviera. It took us four days, and we spent a night sleeping on the beach at San Tropez after arriving at 3 a.m., in the pitch-black. We woke in bright sunshine to the full beauty of the picturesque old

town and before it, the brilliant blue Mediterranean. I left my Scottish friend there and the next day found Marie-France in Nice.

After a very pleasant few days in the south, I moved to Paris with Marie-France and into her apartment. It was then six weeks since I had left Woking and after an initial phone call to tell them I'd arrived in France, I hadn't spoken to my parents. Quite simply, I was petrified that they would plead with me to come home and I wouldn't be able to resist my mother's tears. Plus, there was also the fact that I was now, in mum's and dad's eyes at least, living in sin with a girl.

I left it nine months before I contacted them again, which is one of the great regrets of my life. I had run away from home and left them to go potty with worry. At one point, they told me, they'd even tried to get Interpol to locate me but I somehow managed to elude their clutches.

Cherchez l'Idole

I very quickly adapted to my new life in Paris, though. The restaurants were great, and unlike anything I'd known in England—people sat on the pavement drinking coffee, smoking, watching the world go by in a way that wouldn't occur to anyone in Woking to do. Because the Germans hadn't bombed Paris in the way that London had been, the city seemed to be somehow older and more antiquated than even Soho was at the time. Like Soho, Paris had streets of shops with peeling painted signs, rickety-looking fresh fruit and vegetable tables groaning under the weight of stuff, but the French capital didn't have huge bombed spaces between fantastically ornate buildings, or whole streets of construction work going on. Even the traffic seemed to flow easier than it did in London. Because of her previous success as an actress, Marie-France shopped and ate at upmarket places, and she knew the city really well. I managed to spend a lot of time rooting around in record shops, and in particular a couple of fantastic stores on the Champs-Elysees that used to stock American and British imports. Financially though, I was entirely dependent on Marie-France and she supported me to begin with, and then helped me to find work. Fortunately for me she was pretty well plugged into the Parisian music scene. Through her contacts I got a couple of gigs and

people slowly started to become aware of my name. I was able to play a little bit of traditional Nashville-style country guitar, which was hugely popular in France at the time, and that helped to make my reputation.

I got to play with some of the oddest people, too. There was one guy who called himself and his band Hector and the Mediators. "Mediator" in French means plectrum, so it was Hector and the Plectrums. Hector claimed to be an American (although he was born Jean Pierre Kalfon in Paris) and to have grown up in Louisiana, where he became a big fan of Screaming Jay Hawkins—whose act he was inspired by. Hector looked like Groucho Marx, with a shock of black frizzy hair and goggling eyes, and he branded himself "the Chopin of rock." If nothing else, he was certifiably crazy and in 1965 claimed to have been asked by the French Secret Services to undertake a mission to Israel (in fact he played at the Maxim in Jaffa for a few nights before being sacked for getting too drunk on stage). He was also more of a personality than a singer, but had a certain shall we say, *je ne sais quoi* on stage. Hector got to appear in what became quite a big film in France in 1964, *Cherchez l'Idole*, or *Look for the Idol* as it would be in English, and I recorded a couple of

Hector, whose "Mediators"
I joined in Paris in 1963.

Big brother (and band leader)
Eddie backstage with Sylvie
Vartan, 1964.

songs with him for the soundtrack, and so I appeared in the movie playing guitar on 'Il Faut Saisirsa Chance.' That gig proved to be another significant stepping stone for me.

We filmed the band's scenes for the movie at the famous Olympia Theatre in Paris in early December 1963. That was where all the national and international stars of the day played, and is a classic, grand old music hall that seats three thousand people and has about it an air of refinement. When we went onstage to do our sound check, I happened to notice a guy looking on from the wings. I didn't pay him any mind, but after we had finished filming our bit, he came up to me, introduced himself and asked if I'd like a job. His name was Eddie Vartan and he was elder brother and mentor to Sylvie Vartan, who had become a teenage singing sensation in France and was the female star of the movie.

The Vartans were actually Bulgarian, but the family had emigrated to Paris in 1952, when Sylvie was just seven. Eddie was a fine musician, a trumpet player and arranger, and in 1961 produced his sister's first record, 'Panne d'Essence,' a duet with another French rocker, Frankie Jordan, which was a huge hit in France. After that, the French press dubbed Sylvie "the twisting schoolgirl" and under Eddie's guidance she had gone on to have several hits in her own right, one of which was her version of Ray Charles' 'What'd I Say.'

That's me, behind Sylvie, onstage at the Olympia Theater, Paris, January 1964.

When I said I'd definitely be interested in working with him, Eddie whisked me off to meet Sylvie, which to be frank was a moment of pure ecstasy. Sylvie might have been Bulgarian, but she looked like a classic French beauty: blond-haired, dark-eyed and with pouting, bee-stung lips. Outside of my girlfriend she was the prettiest girl I'd ever laid eyes on, and I was dazzled.

In 2016 the two of us went to lunch and were talking about the old times. I told Sylvie then for the first time how I'd been utterly infatuated with her in those days. She replied, "Oh darling, you should have let on at the time." If I had, though, the whole world I'd just begun to build up would have been brought crashing down around me. Sylvie had just married Johnny Hallyday, the so-called "French Elvis" (and co-star of *Cherchez L'Idole*, along with Charles Aznavour) and who even at that time was a cultural icon in France. Johnny was a very charismatic and powerful guy, and I have no doubt that if there'd been any funny business between Sylvie and me, it wouldn't have gone too well for me.

From that first meeting at the Olympia, Eddie and Sylvie kind of made me one of their family. I spent a lot of time at the family apartment in Paris, having meals cooked for me by their mother in what was a traditional Bulgarian setting. Eddie was also looking for a drummer for Sylvie's band and asked me if I knew of anyone. Tommy Brown, Nero and the Gladiators' drummer, had hooked up with a French girl and moved to Paris after the Gladiators split. After they had recorded an EP of French language versions of songs including Roy Orbison's 'Blue Bayou,' Fats Domino's 'There Goes My Heart Again,' and the Beatles' 'Love Me Do' with Rivers, though. So, I called Tommy and asked him to come down to an audition, and he got the gig, which was very good of me I think, considering he'd had no qualms about abandoning me back in Bordeaux. But then, I never have tended to dwell on things. I'm like my mum in that respect, perhaps a bit too forgiving of other people. And Tommy was such a larger-than-life character, so typical of a drummer, and he was a good man to have around.

It wasn't long after performing
with the Beatles that my hair
started getting longer...

British Invasion

Tommy and I hadn't played more than a handful of gigs with Sylvie when she was booked to appear for 19 days of shows at the Olympia with the Beatles and Trini Lopez. The shows began with a matinee on January 16, 1964, and the Beatles were already by then known as the Fab Four back home in Britain, having hit Number One three times the previous year with 'From Me to You,' 'She Loves You,' and 'I Want to Hold Your Hand.' In fact, they flew straight off from Paris to New York to make that epochal first assault on America. I couldn't believe my good fortune when Eddie told me about the gigs, and was in a kind of dream state for a few days beforehand.

On the first day of their residency, we arrived at the Olympia for sound check to find the Beatles already at work. The initial thing that struck me about them was just how down to earth they all were. They carried their own gear up on to the stage, their amps in hand and guitars strapped on. That opening show passed me by in a blur, I was so nervous. Not that things went smoothly for the Beatles on their first evening show. Just as they were about to start a fuse blew or something and the amps went dead, so Ringo played a drum solo until a new fuse could be fitted. Then there were so many press photographers backstage and on the side of the stage that things got out of hand and punches were thrown as they tried to get a good shot. Paul stopped the show in order to get everyone off stage and settled down. They banned all photographers from backstage after that, which at least made things a little less manic during show times.

Texan rock 'n' roll singer Trini Lopez had just had a massive Number One single with 'If I Had a Hammer,' and he usually played before us and the Beatles. I soon found out that his drummer was also called Mick Jones—or Mickey Jones from Dallas, Texas, as he introduced himself to me. I can remember the two of us having a photograph taken together, both holding our passports open.

Once Trini Lopez's set was over, the curtain would come down and after a short interlude be raised again to reveal Sylvie and her band. It was a typical music hall curtain, made of velvet, and on the third night my guitar got snagged on it as it was being pulled up. It was the electric Gibson SG that my dad had bought me on HP, and the curtain was so heavy, I was near enough lifted off my feet. I loudly exclaimed something as eloquent as, "Oh sh...!" and managed to get myself untangled before too much damage was done. Afterward, in the dressing room, John Lennon came up to me and said, 'Hey lad, we didn't know you were English. Come up for a bevvy with us after the show.'

For the next ten days, John, Paul, George, and Ringo really did make me feel as if I was the fifth Beatle. The four of them were being billeted at the George V hotel, one of the best in Paris, and they had taken over an entire floor. One night after a show we went back to the hotel and sat around in one their rooms, strumming guitars. Paul would play a regular right-hand guitar and then turn it over and play left-handed, and just as well, at that. There was a knock at the door and the hotel's head chef came in wheeling a silver-service trolley. The George V was famed as a five-star, gastronomic wonder, but laid out on this trolley were four dishes of bread and butter pudding and custard. With a flourish, the chef produced four spoons and announced, "Gentlemen, will you please taste. Tonight, I think I have made it *tres bon*."

Apparently, this same scene had been going on for a week. The Beatles had teased the chef that he wouldn't be able to make bread and butter pudding just so and he'd taken up their challenge. The four of them set about tasting their dishes as if they were rare wines, while this poor guy looked on, literally shaking in his boots, waiting to see if it had pleased them. They got up to a lot of silly, stupid stuff like that, just to amuse themselves. It was harmless fun, though, never malicious. The four of them were very charming, but rascals and always wisecracking. They had an aura about them too, most definitely a huge presence. That was clearly as a result of the natural chemistry that they had going on together, but also I think because they understood each other implicitly, having come from the same backgrounds and they'd already been together solidly as a band for almost three years. John, Paul, and George had played music together since 1958. They'd toured constantly, and played up to eight sets a day at the Star Club in Hamburg in 1961, before meeting Brian Epstein and becoming almost a fixture at the Cavern Club in their home town.

Being with them was my first glimpse into the big time and all that went with it if you were a successful young man making music. The reaction to them in Paris was pure madness, just like you see in all of the black-and-white footage of them from the time and with mobs of hysterical girls. I had got myself a pair of Beatles boots and a mop-top haircut, so I blended in with

The Beatles with Sylvie
Vartan at the Olympia,
Paris, January 1964.

Mickey Jones, the
drummer with Trini Lopez,
"threatening" me with a
fire axe, backstage at the
Olympia, Paris, January
1964.

them. Whenever we ran out of the backstage door at the Olympia, and we had to run, all you could hear were girls screaming and crying. The band was being ferried around in a fleet of black Austin Princess cars and we'd all have to dive into the back seats to escape from having the clothes torn from off our backs.

Every moment with them was like being in a scene from *A Hard Day's Night*. If we went out on the town, no sooner would we have sat down in a club than crowds of girls would descend upon our table. One night, I was having a drink and felt something brush against my leg under the table. It doesn't take much imagination to work out what happened next, and soon enough the table was rocking on its legs. By then, I'd also gotten to know quite a few of the local musicians in Paris and I took the Beatles out on another occasion to see a band made up of US servicemen called Rocky Roberts and the Airedales. They played all of the R&B stuff that the Beatles had been listening to, in particular a killer version of Marvin Gaye's 'Can I Get a Witness,' and the lads sat there mesmerized.

By the end of the fortnight, I'd gotten so close to them that I actually fantasized they might take me off to America with them. I felt utterly

depressed the day before they were leaving. We went out to a poky little bar that night because they wanted to play pinball, which they had picked up during their days in Hamburg. Funny enough, all of us had the same kind of cigarette lighter—a gold Dunhill, Marie-France had bought mine for me—and somebody suggested that we swap them as a memento of our time together. We put all of the lighters on top of the pinball machine, mixed them up and then each picked one out at random. Later in the evening, I went to get a drink, put my lighter down on the bar and next thing I knew, it was gone, vanished. I was devastated, because that was my connection to them, the one thing I hoped to keep.

In hindsight though, I think they also left me with a vision, still vague at the time, of what I might go on to do. However brief, the peek that I'd had into their world was extraordinarily intoxicating. I've been asked ever since if they were that good a band and I can honestly say, oh yes, they were. Every night, the curtain would come up and all hell would break loose. I was in heaven just being able to stand at the side of the stage and watch them and see the audience driven to tears once again. I hadn't ever heard a band play like the Beatles.

This Letter to...

Joining Sylvie's band was the beginning of my career as a songwriter. Before then, I had just been playing other people's songs, but playing in cover bands was actually a good training ground. I got a comprehensive education in how to put chord sequences together and how to structure a song. Even if a lot of the time it was done subconsciously, by the time I arrived in Paris I had taken on board a wealth of information that I was now able to put to good use.

Tommy Brown became my writing partner and the first song we composed together was for Sylvie, titled 'Cette Lettre La.' Some 50 years later she told me that it was still one of her favorites, and it was actually a pretty cool song. To write for Sylvie I had to immerse myself in her music a little bit, figure out how her voice would need to sound; writing for other people is like penning a part for an actor. After that first effort, Tommy and I became prolific. We would never spend an indulgent amount of time on one song of course, not like later on when I got used to records taking a whole year to make. Ever since then though, I've always really enjoyed collaborating with other people on songs, because of the constant state of contrast and having to be open to hearing someone else's ideas. It's the same with producing records; I like having someone to bounce ideas off.

At the beginning, Tommy and I would work with a French writer who would translate our lyrics—which is why the record's centerpiece credits a Frenchman as co-writer with Tommy, and not me. We didn't ever sing in French, but there were a bunch of specialists who'd adapt songs for the home market. Inevitably, there were certain quirks to working in a different country. As Tommy and I were English and not able to sight-read music, we initially had difficulty joining the French music publishing organization, which was called SACEM. Eventually, we had to do an audition for them to prove our credentials. They put the two of us in a white-walled room with a tape recorder and told us to write a song, separately. I'd never before written to order, but it only took me about half an hour to prepare a bunch of chords and sing whatever came into my head. We weren't, though, allowed to register as co-writers for some stupid reason or other, so we had to take turns crediting ourselves as the writers on our earliest songs for Sylvie, regardless of how much or little we might each have contributed. At the beginning, we were paid a flat fee for each song but as things started to progress, we did get publishing royalties. A bunch of our songs went on to do pretty well in France, too, so I did alright out of them. That was a heady period for me, being with Sylvie. We traveled around the country, playing everywhere

EPs featuring songs that Tommy
and I wrote for Sylvie, although
all co-credited with Frenchmen.

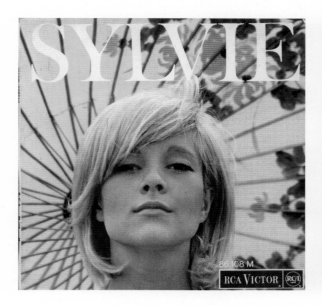

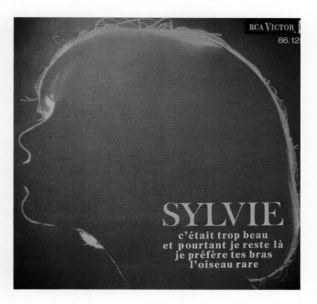

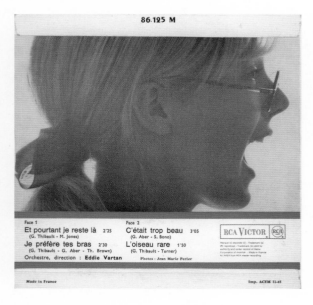

OPPOSITE: The Shirelles,
(L-R) Doris Coley, Shirley
Owens, Beverley Lee,
Addie Harris.
ABOVE: Portrait photo
taken in a room at the
Commodore in 1964.

from the major cities to small rural towns and
open-air fairs. But no matter the size of the place,
the food and wine provided was always incredible.
I felt completely at home, as if this was exactly
where I was supposed to be—at least at that point
in my life.

Early in 1965, with Sylvie's fiancé Johnny Hallyday
doing his National Service in the Army, I went to
New York for the first time with Sylvie to appear
on the *Johnny Carson Show* and a pop show called
Hullabaloo, and it was as weird, wonderful, and
eye-opening as I'd kind of expected. When I first
saw the city, I walked around in a state of awe of
the buildings and streets and almost got a crick
in my neck from always looking up. I understood
then why they were called skyscrapers. But at
street level I noticed that nearly every man seemed
to be wearing a uniform. They wore tight trousers
that stopped above the ankle, white socks and
penny loafers, button-down shirts and tight vests,
and they all had crew cut-hair, which must have
been why plenty of people, when they first saw
us, must have thought we were from another

place—probably Britain, was the most common guess among Americans we met. It didn't take long before we couldn't walk down the street in New York without our being accosted by people asking, "Hey, are you guys with Dave Clark Five?" or, "Are you the Who... the Animals?" On our first day there, a photographer spotted us as we walked along 42nd Street and took us to the Commodore hotel where he had a room and said, "Hey, come upstairs, I've got a studio set up and want to take your picture." Naturally flattered, we went up and he took all these promo photos of us. We must have told him where to send the photos, which duly appeared before we flew back to France.

One night while we were there, our promoter Ivan Mogul drove us up to Harlem to see a show at the legendary Apollo Theatre. Harlem was 99 percent black in those days and when we walked in at first there was a certain tension in the air, but Mogul was well connected enough that it passed, and once the show began all I could concentrate on was the stage. Top of the bill

was Jackie Wilson, but also appearing was the old R&B group The Coasters (who'd had world-wide hits in the late '50s with 'Yakety-Yak' and 'Poison Ivy') and a girl-group, the Shirelles who I was crazy about at the time, as were the Beatles who'd covered their 'Baby, It's You' and 'Boys' on the *Please Please Me* album. After the show, we went backstage, met the Shirelles and invited them out to dinner.

We were staying on the Upper East Side, near Central Park at the Pierre Hotel on East 61st Street. There was a Chinese restaurant near to the hotel where we had eaten dinner most nights. So we took the Shirelles—who were Addie "Micki" Harris, Shirley Owens, Beverly Lee, and Doris Coley—there, but when we walked through the door the manager rushed over and said there were no tables available. The place was clearly half empty. Of course, he had seen that we were with an entourage of black people and didn't want to serve them. That was the first time I'd encountered blatant racism. But we kicked up a big fuss and he finally let us all in to eat.

L'Amitie

Writing songs for Sylvie opened other doors for me, too. I got to be quite friendly with a very well-regarded Parisian photographer, Jean-Marie Périer who had just begun directing a movie called *Tumuc Hamac*, which he hoped to film in the Amazonian region of the title and on Devil's Island. It took a few years to get the movie finished, though, and it wasn't released until 1970. It was a take on the *Papillon* story, in which the convict Henri Charriere's grandson goes on a journey looking for him. Jean-Marie asked Tommy and me to write the score and contribute a couple of songs for the soundtrack. Jean-Marie happened to be the fiancé of Francoise Hardy at the time, and she, like Sylvie, had been having hits in France since the early '60s and from when she was 17. Francoise was a great beauty. Through Jean-Marie, she got to hear the stuff Tommy and I were doing and invited me round to her apartment one afternoon.

That was an encounter to remember. Francoise was just, well, wow! She was dressed in a kind of arty style, all in black, tights, a big long pullover, and with her hair just about down to her derriére. She was breathtakingly sexy. I was barely able to form the words to speak, but I ended up going back a couple of times and Tommy and I came up with a bunch of songs that she sang. In one of her books, she actually describes me as a "charming, sexy young Englishman." If only she'd told me that at the time!

Through Sylvie, I also obviously got to meet Johnny Hallyday who made just as striking an impression on me. I would liken him at the time to being a kind of combination of Elvis and James Dean; he had that sort of magnetic presence. I got to learn from Johnny how he had been playing guitar and performing since he was a child. His Belgian father (whose name was Leon

It seems that I briefly had blond hair and a Warhol-style look in the mid-1960s.

Johnny Hallyday on stage, September 1960. Can you see the Elvis influence?

Smet) and French mother (Huguette Clerc) split up before he was a year old and he went to live with his father's sister, a former silent movie star named Helene Mar. She had two grown-up daughters, Destra and Menen, who were dancers and toured France constantly. By the time Johnny was four years old, Destra was married to an American who used the stage name Lee Hallyday and they more or less adopted him. The Hallydays took him along on tour with them and for the first part of their show dressed him up as a little cowboy and sent him out to sing and play guitar. When Lee became the MC at the Café de Paris, little Johnny was given a regular performing slot and so began his musical career.

Clearly, Elvis was Johnny's idol and he'd taken all his moves from Presley, and after having his first hit in 1960 he never looked back (his 1961 version of 'Let's Twist Again' sold over a million copies in France). In December 1964, though, just like Elvis had done in 1958, Johnny had to do compulsory national service in the army. He was based on the German frontier for most

of his service, at a town called Offenbach near Strasbourg in France, and that year in the army was documented just as avidly as Presley's had been back in the States.

He'd been drafted just after I met him, but we'd hit it off well enough that whenever on leave (which was often) Johnny would join us and Sylvie on stage for a couple of songs if we were performing, and he took me out with him around the clubs of Paris (sometimes he and I would join bands playing at those clubs for a number or two). It was like a repeat of my nights with the Beatles when we were out and about though, since he attracted frenzied attention and hordes of photographers wherever he went. He took me for my first ride on a Harley Davidson bike—at two in the morning, racing through the city streets. I didn't know it at the time, but as well as showing off, he was kind of seducing me away from his wife and into joining his band. And I couldn't help but think, "Well, this could be the life for me."

Go, Johnny, Go!

Johnny was probably a bit of a misogynist, but that was the way things were in those days. In his pursuit of me, and of Tommy, it was as if he were saying to Sylvie, "I'm number one here and I can take what I want." Sylvie wasn't happy about it, to put it mildly, but there was nothing she could do and Johnny was very determined. In the end, he stole virtually her whole band from her.

Those first couple of years I was with Johnny, 1966 and 1967, were breathless. Every day was different, exciting, and I had the experience of traveling around the world for the first time. We went to South America and played in Brazil, Argentina, and Uruguay, before heading to the French West Indies for a week or two and after that to Montreal. On any given day, I wouldn't know what to expect and Johnny was always prone to throw curve balls into a situation. But it was a very glamorous life and I partook fully in every aspect of it. I also got to play with great musicians and to really learn my craft.

Johnny was such a huge star and there had never been anyone like him in France, at least not in rock and roll. He was so much of a trendsetter, he dressed ahead of everyone else in the country and people worshiped him. His shows were maniacal events. Girls would be crying in the front rows, baring their breasts at him and many were apparently orgasmic, too. I mean, you could see them from the stage, they were playing with themselves and in states of ecstasy. It was incredible to witness that level of adulation and it was the same everywhere Johnny went; he would be instantly recognized.

L-R: Me, Tommy Brown
(drums), Johnny Hallyday,
bassist Gérard Fournier
(AKA Papillon), Olympia,
Paris 1967.

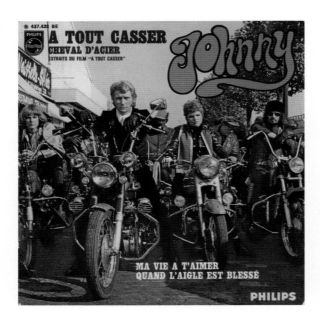

EPs featuring songs
written and arranged by
Tommy and me.

At the point I joined him, Johnny was still mostly playing covers of American-English songs, but singing them in French. I was hired as a guitar player, but that soon changed, when me and Tommy began to write songs for him. On occasion, the three of us would sit down and play together, seeing what came out, though in reality it wouldn't matter whether Johnny was present or not—Tommy and I were still quite naïve, and we accepted the unwritten rule that Johnny be credited on each of our songs as a co-writer, even if he'd had nothing to do with it. We were considered as lucky to have a song on a Johnny Hallyday record, because it was guaranteed to sell and that was supposed to soften the blow of foregoing a third of our royalties. It turned out to be a pretty fair swap, over time.

Gradually, we began to replace the covers in Johnny's live set with our original songs. Eventually, Johnny allowed me to also start producing his records with Tommy. That was the key to my becoming more of an all-round musician, writer, arranger, and producer and for that I am indebted to him. I had picked up a lot of knowledge on the technical side from being in the studio with Eddie Vartan, but nevertheless it was still daunting to be at the head of this quite sprawling band the Blackburds, which comprised trumpet players, trombonists, and saxophonists. Somehow, even though I wasn't a trained musician, I managed to earn their respect. All of the records that I made with Johnny were finished quickly, in three to four weeks, tops, and the studios in Paris at that time

were quite sophisticated. They had the most up-to-date American equipment such as stand-up Ampeg tape machines with eight available tracks. But France, being a very bureaucratic kind of society, required all of the people who worked in studios would have to wear white coats which made them look like laboratory technicians or pharmacists, and it made the studios seem quite sterile environments. Then there were the unions. When my name started to get around town, quite a few of the native musicians became resentful that there was an Englishman running sessions in Paris. They sort of ganged up against me and fed bogus information to the musicians' union, which they acted on and at one point it got to be really difficult for me to work.

There wasn't an open-door policy for foreigners to be able to live and work in France; eventually you had to have a permit. I didn't, which began to make things very difficult for me until Johnny intervened. He did a deal to get me the permit, but how he managed it was never made exactly clear-cut. The pay-off though was that we had to go to Corsica, right up into the mountains, and do a show. Now, Corsica is to France what Sicily is to Italy, and this whole escapade was just like that scene in *The Godfather II* when Vito Corleone goes back to his home town. After we had lugged all of our gear up to this rustic village in the mountains, Johnny paid a visit to the minister for that part of the island. He pretty much had to kiss his hand and then we played for the locals in the main square.

Duck!

During my time with Johnny we had quite a few run-ins with the French Mafia, and different gangsters. There was also a section of the French press that delved into every nook and cranny of Johnny's private life and wouldn't let up, which became very difficult for him to handle. One of the big stories came to be about Johnny's relationship with his estranged father. His dad was basically an alcoholic bum—a comedic singer and dancer who traveled with circuses across Europe—and he had abandoned him as a child. Naturally, Johnny had cut all ties to him. Eventually, his dad started to complain to the press though, and it blew up into this big tabloid story, the thrust of which was that Johnny was being cruel to his father, which in the more traditional areas of French was very much frowned upon.

So Johnny was closely watched by a press eager to get any story on him they could, but that didn't stop him from doing pretty much what he wanted, no matter how impetuous or dangerous it was. On one occasion when we were playing on the French Riviera, we were larking about during the day and there's a photograph of Tommy and me with Johnny, where we're lifting him up by his arms and legs, all smiles, looking as if we're about to throw him in the Med, and it was taken on the seafront the afternoon that we arrived in Cannes. That picture doesn't give any clue as to the madness that was to follow that day, though. Later on in the evening, Johnny called down to my room at our hotel and asked me if I'd like to go with him on a little ride along the coast road to Nice. He had just bought himself a brilliant white convertible Bentley and we went swanning off in it together looking for fun and high jinks.

Johnny Hallyday with one of his luxury cars in
the late 1960s: a Lamborghini Miura.

Tommy and me about to throw Johnny into the Med on the Cote d'Azur in France, 1967. Oh, the madness that followed on that day...

We went to a casino in Nice and then on to this very sleazy-looking bar; all of the women in the place were clearly hookers. The two of us were seated at the bar, chatting the girls up, when a guy, one of their pimps, tried to butt in. Johnny asked the guy to stop pushing, but he wouldn't quit bugging us. So Johnny did what he was liable to do at any time, which was to turn round and lay the guy out with a single punch. Pandemonium broke out in the club, with guns pulled, and shots fired. Naturally, Johnny and I high-tailed it out of there, dived into the Bentley, and tore off down the street, wheels spinning and screeching.

That, though, wasn't the end of the drama that evening. We got back to Cannes and pulled up outside the hotel, right across the road from which there was a Corsican pizza parlour. The second we stepped out of the car, a guy burst out of the pizza place, waving a gun around and shouting at Johnny, "You bastard, leaving your father like that!" He then started firing shots into the air. Johnny and I raced into the hotel and hid behind the reception desk. Everyone else scattered—all of the staff and other guests—and that was how our night on the town ended and it was just one of many similar incidents. I suppose that I got quite hooked on the excitement.

Johnny and I used to hang out at weekends when we weren't working, and one Sunday afternoon we didn't have much to do, so he said, "Let's just chill, watch a movie." I went to his place, he had a super-8 projector ready, but was in a dressing gown when he let me in, and said he was going to have a bath, I should make myself

at home, and, "If anyone knocks, let them in." So I started the movie but an hour into it, Johnny's still in the bath and there's a rap on the door. I pause the movie, open the door and there stands Brigitte Bardot, right in front of me. Now, you have to understand, with my love of all things French at the time, and all women French... I was somewhat stunned to find her there. She wasn't alone, either, but with a friend who was equally as stunning. They came in, Johnny came out of the bathroom and... we had a nice dinner and lovely evening.

Hey, Joe

Not too long after I started running Johnny's Blackburds band for him, we went to London to try and recruit Brian Auger and Julie Driscoll for a two-week tour of northern France that we had booked. We went to see Brian play at a club called the Cromwellian on Cromwell Road. By chance, Chas Chandler and Jimi Hendrix happened to be at the next table. That night Jimi got up and sat in with Brian's band Trinity and basically destroyed the place, tore it apart with some fantastic playing. After he'd finished and the hub-bub had cooled down, we got Jimi to come over to our table and have a drink. Johnny introduced himself and we learned that Chas wanted to get Jimi out on some kind of tour before he began to properly drill his own band, the Experience.

Brigitte Bardot smiles as
Johnny serenades her for
the camera.

That's me, shaking the tambourine to the right of Jimi Hendrix, on the tour we did together in 1966. Julie Driscoll is singing in front of me.

Back we went to northern France, and with Jimi in tow. A friend of Johnny's, a guy called Long Chris, opened up those shows. Jimi was second on the bill, and then Brian and Julie. The Blackburds would come out and do a short set and then Johnny would join us and finish the show. But really, Jimi was the big talking point. We were playing in towns like Lille and Lens, which were nowhere near as cosmopolitan as Paris, and Jimi was beyond the limits of those people's experience. A black guy playing rock 'n' roll—they just didn't know what to do when he began playing, so they mostly sat there open-mouthed, staring up at him. There wasn't even a whisper when he was playing, not on any night of the tour.

Jimi got up and jammed with us on a few nights and taught me how to play 'Hey Joe.' He was so cool, just a lovely, sweet guy. I think he was smoking quite a bit of dope at the time, which I hadn't encountered before then; he was so mellow. Otherwise, all he did was play his guitar or comb his hair. He took great care over his appearance. All of us on the tour were shell-shocked by how this laid-back guy was transformed on stage; he blew everybody away with technique and volume. I don't know if watching him was more exciting or intimidating, but I'd never seen the like of him, that's for sure. One night, he helped me to re-adjust my guitar, and set it up to be just as he played his Strat. I didn't re-tune it for a couple of days at least, because I didn't want to inadvertently change anything. The day Jimi taught me 'Hey Joe' I went to a club in St Germain des Prés called Le Bilboquet after our gig. It was an after-hours favorite of musicians. Dave Gilmour (later of Pink Floyd) and Rick Wills were playing in the house band there, and I'd gotten to know them well, and even helped them out financially a bit. I asked David if I could jam on a new song—they had probably only heard it on the radio a couple of times, but they willingly agreed. It went down very well, and we played on till dawn. When I explained how it had come about, they were green with envy!

In March 1967, Johnny played a month-long residency at the Olympia, which was a huge deal for the time. We did six shows a week, one night off. On one of the nights off, the Stax Review were booked into the theatre, fronted by Otis Redding. The evening of the show, Steve Cropper was having problems with his amp so I lent him mine, which I was thrilled to do as you can imagine. Steve then introduced me to Otis, who was another sweet, sweet guy.

I'd had the idea to make more of a soul-influenced record with Johnny, so I floated the idea to Otis that the two of them sing a duet on one of his songs. The next day, we went into the studio, Johnny, Otis, me and the Blackbirds, where we cut a version of 'Try a Little Tenderness.' I don't know that Johnny ever released it, but the magic of that day was seeing Otis work at close quarters. Our version of the song was sung in French, so it obviously wasn't going to rock quite like the original, but Otis took the time to teach Johnny to phrase the way he did and told us where his style of singing had come from, the whole history of the blues. For the session, I was at the mixing desk and Otis stood behind me. He watched and listened for a while, and then said, "You guys, you hear things different to me. You hear it on the one and I hear it on the in between." And if you listen to any of Otis' songs, that's the rhythm that you're hearing. That whole Stax scene was a major influence on me, and to be up close to Otis and effectively Booker T and the MGs was an amazing privilege. I got to see a whole bunch of other great artists in Paris, too, like James Brown, Sly and the Family Stone, the Everly Brothers, Little Richard, and many, many more.

State of Micky and Tommy

Several of the best British musicians of the period came over to do sessions with Johnny, basically because for them it was a free weekend in Paris. I suggested that Jimmy Page come over and record with us in 1967. He arrived with the great producer-engineer Glyn Johns, who had already by then recorded the Stones, the Who, the Kinks, and the Small Faces, among others.

John Paul Jones played some sessions in France for me, as did Ronnie Lane, Steve Marriott, and Peter Frampton. Marriott in particular was great—he was only a little guy, but a proper white soul man and a totally explosive performer. Back then, life in Paris was never dull.

There was another side to working with Johnny, of course, because like all such huge stars he sometimes put his own well-being above others. That was certainly the case when Tommy and I went off to do our own thing, even though Johnny initially encouraged us to do so. Once we'd developed the Blackburds into a really tight-sounding band, Johnny suggested we record something ourselves. The two of us were writing fairly productively at the time, and so it seemed like the logical next step. Initially, we put out a song under the name of Nimrod, but quickly changed that to the State of Mickey and Tommy.

The State of Micky and Tommy, playing our
solo spot before Johnny headlines, 1967.

L-R: Before we became
State of Micky and Tommy,
we released as single as
Nimrod. We also wrote
and produced Ronnie Bird.

Under that handle, we recorded English versions
of several songs we had originally written for
Johnny. I suppose the best-known of these would
be 'Frisco Bay,' which Tommy and I cut in 1967.
It had quite a psychedelic feel to it—I'd heard
the Byrds and Buffalo Springfield by then and
definitely felt connected with all of that music
coming out of California. It was a Top 20 hit in
France. Johnny was in hippy mode at the time,
too, and we had some pretty scary outfits—
Afghan coats, Edwardian military jackets with
braid ands brass buttons, that sort of thing.
We'd been watching American and British bands
changing their look, heard them sounding
different and we took from them bits and songs
that really moved us. Johnny wanted to do a
cover of the Buffalo Springfield song, 'For What
It's Worth,' which was a huge hit in 1967, for
instance, as well as covering Stax songs.

Tommy and I enjoyed a certain amount of
success together over the next three or four
years after 'Frisco Bay' was a hit, but Johnny still
made sure to keep us under his wing. I think he
thought that the State of Micky and Tommy might
be the end of us being with him. He was a little
bit possessive, let's put it that way. I'm still not
sure if it was a good or bad thing that we didn't
strike out on our own entirely, but Tommy and
I wrote some good songs and got given a lot of
encouragement because we were signed to the
same label as Johnny—Philips.

After the release in France of the 'Frisco Bay'
EP, Tommy and I flew over to New York with
Johnny. I'd organized for him to record with
some of the best session guys in town, and at
the same time Tommy and I got to do some
demos for Mercury Records. That didn't lead to
anything, unfortunately, but New York in 1967

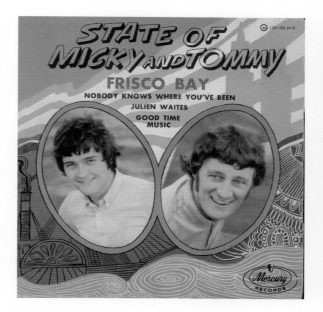

Our biggest hit EP, which
was very much a product
of the times (1967). Copies
of it are apparently now
very valuable...

was a truly wild place to be. We were staying off Broadway near Times Square and there were all kinds of hustlers out on the streets. I remember people gawking at Tommy and me, because we still had our Beatles haircuts. Girls would chase after us shouting, "Hey! Are you guys with Herman's Hermits?" It had only been a couple of years since I'd last been in the city, but it had changed, or perhaps I had, and I was seeing parts of it that I'd missed on my first visit. Being with Johnny instead of with Sylvie and Eddie made a huge difference to where we went and who we saw, of course. Even given that we were meeting with musicians who were hip, on the streets the preppy look had mostly gone, and men in New York were no longer wearing that uniform, even on Madison Avenue. There were plenty of hippies about, but even working men's hair was longer and their clothes looser. In Paris the students still looked as if it was 1957, not

'67 and generally had short hair and still wore jackets and ties, or roll-neck sweaters and duffle coats. No one in Paris would have thought about walking the city streets without shoes, but there were several young men and women whom I saw doing that in New York. The generation gap had widened to the point of there being two distinct species of New Yorker, it seemed to me: the young and everyone else. The thing was that the "young" were also getting older, and it wasn't just teenagers or people in their early 20s who were dressing and acting differently. In New York 30-somethings were adopting the hippy look and slang, and you'd hear people calling each other "man" in diners and restaurants alike. The world changed far more rapidly in New York than it did in Paris, or at least it seemed that way in 1967. Within six months, though, that would all change.

Noir Est Noir

In May 1968, there was a general strike in France and student riots in Paris, which brought the entire country to a standstill for days at a time. I was living just down the road from the epicenter of the main conflict in Place Saint Michel at the time. On May 6th an estimated 20,000 students and supporters marched through the area, protesting the government's closure of the city university. That was a terrifying experience: the students threw up barricades across the street, there were petrol bombs going off and in response the police fired rubber bullets, and baton-charged the marchers.

It was complete mayhem. I'd never seen a full-scale riot before; it was a total shock seeing so much raw anger and violence happening on the street where I lived. The government basically gave the special riot squad of the French police, the CRS, *carte blanche* against the marchers, and they were a mean bunch. More than once I had to run the gauntlet of the police and students to get into my building, so after a few days I fled to London for three or four weeks, until it was safe to go back to Paris.

Blackburds, (L-R) Jean Tosan, me, Tommy Brown, Papillon, 1968.

The streets around my
apartment looked like a
war zone in May, 1968.

In 1968 I was most likely regarded as being a part of the anti-establishment in France because of my work with Johnny. He was seen very much as a rebellious, anti-establishment figure in France and he quite often agreed to perform at events for the Communist Party and to appear at huge open-air rallies—in 1966 we played a big outdoor gig in Communist Czechoslovakia, for instance. But to be honest, it was all a little bit manufactured on his part. He certainly wasn't a communist; none of us were. We were essentially good-time capitalists, enjoying all of the rewards that pop music success brought us, which included traveling the world, of course.

Glyn Johns and I had become quite friendly while working together in Paris in 1967, and late the following year I took Johnny over to London with me to work with Glyn on a bunch of songs we'd just then written. One afternoon at the studio in London, Glyn beckoned me into this little mix room and said, "I'm going to play you something—tell me what you think." It was the opening five tracks of the first Led Zeppelin album and, my God, they just destroyed me. Hardly anyone else outside of Glyn, the four members of Zeppelin and their manager Peter Grant had heard these songs at the time. They were so dark, loud, nasty and plain awesome that I was left quivering. That was a real revolution for me. Jimmy was a big researcher of guitar sounds and of new ways of recording the

guitar, and in that respect at least he became a significant influence on my own playing.

As the 1960s came to a close we were all trying to find our way in a new and rapidly developing musical landscape. The psychedelia of '67 gave way to a heavier blues sound in 1968, and 1969 really belonged to Led Zeppelin, as far as I was concerned.

Released in November 1970, *Vie* didn't sound like the emerging sound of heavy metal. Black Sabbath had released their debut album in February, and along with *Led Zep II*, which had been released at the end of 1969 and *Led Zep III* (October 1970) it sounded to me as if rock music had become something different, and particularly British. Which is why I was happy that we recorded the next album in London, at Olympic Studios, where the Stones and Led Zep had been working. I was also encouraged to find that we were to work with a man named Gary Wright, who'd recently disbanded Spooky Tooth in order to go solo. I liked him and his songs, some of which had been translated into French by a guy named Philippe Labro, who also adapted John Fogerty's 'Fortunate Son' and Leon Russell's 'Delta Lady' for the album. The backing singers were superb, the best working in the UK at the time: Nanette Workman, Doris Troy, and Madeline Bell. Stones' horn players Bobby Keys and Jim Price also worked on the album, which

was titled *Flagrant Délit* and released in June, 1971.
I didn't know it at the time, but it was to be the last
album I'd make with Johnny.

Late in 1971, Johnny was invited to Africa to play a
couple of shows. The first of these was in Zaire, as it
had just become, and had been organized by someone
high up in the country's government. This was three
years before Muhammad Ali and George Foreman's
famous "Rumble in the Jungle" fight, and we played
at the same stadium in the capital city, Kinshasa, in
which they were to box. "Stadium" is something of a
grandiose description for that venue though, since it
was so ramshackle it looked as if it had been knocked
together with a hammer and nails and had a dirt pitch
that was more like a ploughed field.

The show was good, though, and our next stop was to
be Cameroon. The government in Zaire had arranged

for us to have the loan of a private jet to take us on
to Cameroon, which was just as well since following
the show we were up all night drinking and hadn't
slept. When we landed in Douala, Johnny went on
ahead of the rest of us to the hotel. I made it into
the second car, so arrived no more than 20 minutes
after him, but that had given Johnny enough time
to cause an international incident. Apparently, an
African gentleman had tried to push in front of him
at the check-in desk and Johnny had decked him.
Unfortunately, the guy turned out to be president of
the Central African Republic and on a state visit.

I remained blissfully unaware that there had been
any trouble for several hours, since I picked up my
key and headed straight out with four guys from the
band and some friends from Paris who were also
in town. We went to a party at a ranch house out in
the countryside, and there was a big old barbeque

OPPOSITE: (L-R) John
Paul Jones, Robert Plant,
Jimmy Page, and John
Bonham appearing at
London's Marquee Club in
the fall of 1968, billed as
The New Yardbirds.
ABOVE: In the studio with
Johnny Hallyday (still
playing my Epiphone Les
Paul), 1969.

Security at the Kinshasa
Stadium was provded by
the military.

thrown for us by a local guy who my Parisian friends had gotten to know. It was all very nice, and quite exotic, until we were interrupted by the shrill sound of a police siren. It was a black Mariah and you could see it approaching from miles off—it stirred a cloud of dust along the road. When it pulled up outside the gate, four armed policemen jumped out, one of them shouting, "Where are the Johnny Hallyday people?"

Our host tried to hide us, and herded us into a barn-like building, but one of the police spotted him and they all burst in after us, waving guns. All of us from Johnny's band were arrested on the spot and taken straight to the city jail. On route, we passed the airport and I saw our plane taking off. Of course, Johnny was on board—the bastard. We were kept in jail, roped together on a wooden bench, for four days. I only had on a pair of swim shorts and a T-shirt, but I had a camera in the shorts, which I didn't dare bring out. There was no food or drink offered to us, except for water, which none of us trusted the look of, and a batch of rock-hard

buns. I tried to ask the officer in charge, a singularly brutal-looking individual, to call the British or French ambassador on our behalf, but he simply replied, "He not there."

As if to add to the surreality of our situation, after a few hours of being chained to the bench a swarm of locusts descended on the building. For three or four hours we'd heard a buzzing sound which grew in intensity, until all of a sudden these voracious insects invaded the jail in a huge cloud. They got everywhere. You had to put your hands over your mouth just to be able to catch a breath of air. The following day, there was a break-out from the prison. A group of ten or so young lads managed to pry open their cell door and made off across the rooftops. The police hunted them down within hours, though.

These kids couldn't have been more than 16, and they were brought back to the jail tethered between two poles like animals, and set down in front of us. Then three or four police officers started beating them to a pulp with baseball bats. This went on for four or five minutes; the kids were wailing in pain. We could see them being cut open but didn't dare do a thing. They were yelling out to us, "When you get back to France, tell people what is going on here."

Finally though, two men from the English and French embassies turned up at the jail. The British diplomat had a double-barrelled name, like Compton-Browne or something, and he'd just returned from being on safari. It took them another day to secure our release and even then the police tried to intimidate us. We were driven back to the airport to take a flight to Kinshasa and twice they trooped us up onto the plane, only to haul us off again, before they eventually let us depart.

When I caught up with Johnny again I told him straight, "Boy, you left us in such a big pile of shit." He just sort of shrugged and said, "Oh, sorry." It didn't even register with him, which left me feeling quite depressed. I had led quite the charmed life up till then, but I had often wondered when it might stop. The African misadventure was the starting point, but as it happened, my time in France was really brought to an end one day on a golf course.

Johnny heads toward the stage in Kinshasa.

Long, Long Way from Home

Do I look uncertain in this
photo? Taken in about
1970.

By this time I had been living in Paris for seven years and had put down roots. While Marie-France and I didn't stay the distance, I had met another beautiful French girl, Babette, and fell very much in love. We were married and had a son together in July 1969, who we named Roman. I had enjoyed the fruits of my collaboration with Tommy Brown, and been able to get a place in Paris and rent a house in Normandy, too. I was seeing the world with Johnny and the Blackburds and to all intents my life appeared to be blessed.

Appearances can be deceiving, though, and I felt that my life was anything but perfect. Professionally I felt as if I was stuck in a rut. I'd begun to find the music I was making in France limiting and as a result had stopped writing songs. Johnny was busy making an album titled *Country, Folk, Rock*, part of it in LA where he used local musicians (including the almost legendary Carol Kaye on bass). Personally, I was in even worse shape. The jet-set lifestyle with Johnny had started to take a physical toll on me. I had become something of an alcoholic, although like most people back then, I didn't realize I had a problem. Worse still, my marriage was floundering. Babette and I loved each other, and indeed we do to this day, but we just couldn't live together.

It all came to a head for me one summer's afternoon while at the place in Normandy, just after *Country, Folk, Rock* had come out, the first of Johnny's albums for five years on which I hadn't taken a leading role. I was a golf fanatic and had gone out to play a round on the local course. I was on the sixth tee, had hit a couple

of balls and was looking forward to getting back to the clubhouse for the 19th hole, when I was stopped dead in my tracks by a single stark thought: "Where the hell is my life going?" I felt constrained somehow, like I'd gotten to the furthest point I could in France. I loved the country, and Paris in particular, but felt as if there was something missing from my life. I was 27 years old, comfortably off, and had a secure job which, in France at least, was the equivalent of being the band leader for Elvis. But right then, it simply wasn't enough.

What does that say about me? Well, I have always been restless, and had a certain curiosity about life and love and music. I suppose I'm a bit of a seeker, which was what had taken me to France in the first place. Some seven years after the event, I was increasingly thinking back to those glorious few days that I spent with the Beatles, and wondering why I had never had a band of my own. I guess self-esteem and pride was also a part of it, too. The reality was that the Blackburds belonged to Johnny and he could do with us as he wished. So it was, I realized, that I wanted to find out if I was meant for something more.

As luck would have it, no sooner had I returned to Paris from Normandy than an opportunity presented itself. One night I fell into a conversation with the producer, Jimmy Miller. By then Jimmy had cut *Beggars Banquet* and *Let It Bleed* with the Rolling Stones, as well as a bunch of records with Traffic and the Blind Faith album with Clapton, Steve Winwood, and Ginger Baker. So when he expressed an opinion about music, I thought it was worth hearing. He suggested to me that I give a good friend of his named Gary Wright a call. Since I already knew Gary, I was delighted to make contact.

An expat American, Gary was a highly talented musician, a pianist, singer, and songwriter who'd trained as a doctor in the US before finishing in Berlin, in 1966. Rather than go back to New York and work as a doctor though, Gary formed a band in Germany called the New York Times and met Jimmy when they got the gig opening up a show in Norway for Traffic. At the same show Gary also met Chris Blackwell, the founder of Island Records, who persuaded him to move to England to form a new band. Once settled in London, Gary got together with a singer named Mike Harrison, drummer Mike Kellie, bassist Greg Ridley, and guitarist Luke Grosvenor from a band called the VIPs who'd recently lost keyboard player Keith Emerson to The Nice, and decided to call themselves Art. Their debut album, *Supernatural Fairy Tales*, came out in 1967 on Island. Six months later they became Spooky Tooth and chose to have both Gary and Mike play keyboards, since no one else was doing that at the time. They made a couple of really good records with Jimmy (*It's All About* in 1968 and *Spooky Two* in 1969), but after Island chose to release an album by French synth player Pierre Henry that the band had played back up on as a joint Spooky Tooth-Henry album (titled *Ceremony*), Gary left the band for a solo career. Spooky Tooth made one album without him (*The Last Puff*) and then split up. In 1970 he released a solo album titled *Extraction* on A&M and also became featured pianist on George Harrison's first solo album, *All Things Must Pass*, which I'd loved. In order to promote *Extraction* Gary had formed a band called Wonderwheel, who he'd then used on the follow-up album, *Footprint*, which was to be released in November, 1971.

Both Gary and I shared a number of musical influences, including Ray Charles, Jerry Lee Lewis, Elvis, and of course the Beatles. So, with the added bonus of Jimmy's recommendation I went over to London to meet with Gary and he told me that Chris Blackwell had asked him to reform Spooky Tooth. Gary could choose whomever he wanted to be in the band and offered me a slot. I was delighted, because although they had never outgrown being a cult band, Spooky Tooth had a really good reputation among musicians. There were a lot of soul influences in their sound, which I liked, and they had something of a Righteous Brothers vibe with two lead singers, a low tenor, and high falsetto. Their original guitarist, Luther Grosvenor, was also such a great player that I felt honored to be asked to step into his shoes—he'd gone to join Stealer's Wheel and then Mott the Hoople (using the pseudonym Ariel Bender).

It didn't take me long to mull over Gary's offer. When I returned to Paris, I asked to see Johnny for a chat, and told him that I'd been asked to join this band, and that I was very appreciative of everything that he had done for me, but that I felt it was time to move on. I think he was shocked; his face went white, and he certainly hadn't seen it coming. It wasn't just Johnny that I was leaving behind of course, there was Tommy too, and that was tough in a different way.

Then there was the most difficult parting of them all, from Babette and Roman. She and I were heading for a divorce, which obviously caused a lot of pain and upheaval, but at the time I was being pulled in another direction. I felt as though Spooky Tooth was a serious opportunity for me, an unmissable one, and so I moved back to England on my own.

Appearing on a live German
television show with Spooky
Tooth (that's me far left, the
singer is Mike Harrison),
1973.

Look at those sideburns!
Must be the early 1970s.

Times Have Changed

The Britain that I'd left eight years previously was a very different place to the one I found on my return. For an idea of how different it was, and how sometimes I felt back then, it's worth watching a BBC television series from 1973 called *Whatever Happened to the Likely Lads*, written by Dick Clement (who later became a good mate) and Ian La Frenais, it was a sequel to their 1966 series *The Likely Lads*. In it one of the original "likely lads" (Terry) returns to his native North East after spending five years stationed in Germany in the army. His former best mate Bob has the job of integrating Terry back into British culture, which has changed enormously since Terry's been away. Terry's short back and sides haircut and mid-sixties narrow suit is in stark contrast to Bob's over-the-collar length coiffed hair, wide-lapeled and mightily flared trouser suits, for a start. I hadn't been as closed off to the developments in music and fashion as Bob had, of course, but the French were generally a few years behind in cultural matters. Everyday fashion in the UK was distinctly different to that of France, and the sight of burly, hairy men wearing stack-heeled shoes, jewelry, bright-colored clothes, and feathered haircuts was usually restricted to fashionable nightclubs in Paris or on the Cote. In England though, men who drove lorries, built houses or worked the docks were dressed up like that for a pub crawl in Portsmouth town center on a Saturday night.

Glam rock was really taking off in a big way. Bands who had previously been considered as members of a certain musical type had switched to being Glam rockers and wearing glitter everywhere, following the success of T. Rex (who I'd last seen as Tyrannosaurus Rex, a hippy duo playing acoustic guitars, bells and bongos) in the pop charts. Now people who'd been mini-Elvis's back in 1962 like Paul Raven and Shane Fenton had been made over into Gary Glitter and Alvin Stardust—although both were still wearing Elvis-like outfits on stage, only glitzier versions—and were becoming proper pop stars. A group of former skinheads called Slade had decided to grow their hair and get glittered up with great success, and a former bubblegum pop act called Sweetshop had dropped the "shop" and become one of the biggest Glam bands around.

The sound of Glam wasn't a million miles away from that of the kind of music which interested me more, and which was being played by the same guitarists who I'd come up with in the pre-Beatles days. Glam used almost old-fashioned rock 'n' roll riffs and classic song structure, all driven by loud and often dirty-sounding guitars—which were in fact almost as loud as those of the likes of Ritchie Blackmore's Deep Purple, who were becoming huge in the wake of Jimmy Page's Zeppelin. Jeff Beck's own group was conquering America, following in the footsteps of Eric Clapton, whose Derek & The Dominoes had become massive with the release of *Layla and Other Love Songs* in 1970. In the UK even groups who were supposedly anti-single oriented, like Deep Purple and Curved Air had enjoyed hit singles—the former with "Black Night" which made number 2 on the UK charts in the summer of 1970, and the latter with "Back Street Luv," which made number 4 a year later.

Of course, since I'd been in France the world had lost many great rock stars—Jimi Hendrix, Janis Joplin, and Jim Morrison for a start. Plus, the Beatles had officially split up, and amazingly Ringo had been the most immediately successful of the band with four straight top ten single hits between 1971 and 1973. Paul had only managed three out of eight, John two, and George just the one.

The music scene was generally incredibly vibrant, with bands reinventing themselves (the Stones switched from being a singles band to an albums act, for instance) and the emergence of "new" styles of music. While the soul scene continued there was a new dance sound coming from the US and UK, called disco. Since 1968 the "rock" scene had sprouted new sub-genres, such as Progressive Rock and Heavy Metal and they were thriving as the 1970s got underway. Along with increased success, rock guitarists were becoming as well known as the singers in bands, and in a few cases they were deified— "Clapton Is God" said graffiti on a wall near Islington tube station in London, and music papers were eager to report that it was true. The names of Page, Beck, Blackmore, the Allmans, Johnny Winter, Alvin Lee, Paul Kossoff, and Rory Gallagher were almost equally as revered as Clapton. It was a great time to be playing music, and England—I hoped—was

going to be a great place to begin a new musical chapter in my life.

To begin with I went to live in Portsmouth where Dad had moved with Mum, in order to take a job in the personnel department of the NAAFI, and to be close to his parents (who still had an Anderson shelter with a corrugated tin roof in their garden in 1972, by the way). It was a difficult time for me being there, of course. I'd experienced all this opulence being around Johnny and very much liked that luxurious life, but now I was starting over again. I also missed Babette and Roman terribly. For a while, I kind of became reclusive. I bought a small boat and learned to tinker with the engine. I even slept on board, which was not as romantic as it sounds, since the boat was usually moored on mud in Portsmouth harbor. I did occasionally take it for a spin around the harbor though, or at least I did until one day it almost capsized in a fairly mild storm. I had Roman and a couple of his cousins with me, and we were just puttering when a wind came up which created some small whitecaps. But they were enough to make my boat roll badly enough that I thought it would capsize— having the kids there, I was genuinely scared, so I didn't do that again.

Yet, being alone in England I did start to write songs again,

Back in England, in the early 1970s, looking only slightly Glam.

In 1963 he was Shane
Fenton, ten years later he
was Alvin Stardust.
OPPOSITE: Mickey Finn
and Marc Bolan (left);
once a Mod, then a hippy,
by 1971 he was a Glam
superstar with T. Rex.

although only the music initially, and in that regard Gary was a big help. He had always been the main writer in Spooky Tooth, and I respected him and liked his style; he was a sophisticated, intelligent guy, good company, and the whole band was much more evolved creatively than anything I had been involved with up to that point. I got a lot of encouragement from him to contribute to the writing, which was important to me. I was battling low self-esteem—a problem that has affected me quite a lot in my life and career. I don't know what first brought it about, even my closest family have never understood it, but it was there from an early age.

I'd been able to hide it pretty much in Paris, having learned from Johnny how to act out a role,

how to project a certain presence, and to make myself seem assured. Before that in England though, there was one instance in particular, when I crumbled prior to playing a gig in Manchester with Nero and the Gladiators. I was backstage and the guitarist with another band on the bill was warming up. He was an unbelievably fast player and doing all these complex scales. He seemed to me so much better than I was, and I had a terrible anxiety attack. As it happened, we went down really well that night and his band got a miserable reception, but I was nonetheless shocked by how I'd been affected.

My self-esteem improved quite a bit in November 1971 though, when Gary asked me to accompany him as part of Wonderwheel on a promotional

trip to America. While we were in New York, Gary and I hooked up with George Harrison, who was still married to Patti Boyd at the time and Ravi Shankar was also on the scene. We played two nights at The Bitter End on Bleeker Street with the comedian Albert Brooks (40 years later I like to kid him about being the support act for my band, which had a Beatle in it), and George asked us to guest with him on the late night ABC live broadcast *Dick Cavett Show*. My standout memory of that day was that I turned up at the studios in a T-shirt with Coca-Cola's old "Coke" logo emblazoned across it, which the producers determined was a drug endorsement. I really wasn't being a smart-arse, but nevertheless they made me take it off before I was even allowed onto the set. That week was the first time I'd

seen George since the Olympia in Paris, ten years beforehand, but he remembered me and we had a good reminisce about it.

Back in England and with Wonderwheel being retired in favor of Spooky Tooth, things gradually came together for me with the band. When you first join a group, it takes a little while to figure out the chemistry between every member, what the hierarchy is—and also, just how many drugs there are likely to be flying around. Until my mid-20s I didn't do many drugs, just a couple of pills to keep me awake, usually Bennies or Dexedrine. But different kinds of drugs were more prevalent in Spooky Tooth, and they were a part of the overall process. Even with that being the case though, I started to feel as if I was regaining

OPPOSITE: (L-R) Gary
Wright, George Harrison,
and me playing live on
America's *Dick Cavett
Show* in November 1971,
not looking Glam.
ABOVE: The Sweet looked
like builders in fancy
dress, but were hugely
successful pop stars in
1972.

some mental stability, which was most definitely appreciated after all the craziness that had gone on during my time with Johnny.

I certainly developed as a musician in the first few months with the band, and bought my first Gibson Les Paul guitar in London. I'd never played one before, but that was to become my signature model. I also got a hold of an Ampeg amplifier and started to get more into sustained playing settings—feedback basically, which I'd first heard coming from Hendrix.

However, I didn't get to contribute any songs to the first album I made with Spooky Tooth. From September 1972, we were at the Island

recording studio in London, working on *You Broke My Heart So… I Busted Your Jaw*, which came out at the start of 1973, and was made up of tracks Gary had originally prepared for a solo album. It wasn't a band record in that sense—a lot of the recording had been done with Wonderwheel in Devon for an album that was, funnily enough, to be titled *Ring of Changes*. Still, on release *You Broke My Heart…* was received well enough by critics and fans, and it seemed to give us a platform from which we could build. There was one track in particular that I was proud of, 'Cotton Growing Man,' on which it seemed to me that my playing had gone up to another level. I was happy in the band and there was obviously more to come from us.

Spooky Tooth, circa March
1973, in Windsor Great
park, for some reason.
(L-R) Chris Stewart, Gary
Wright, Mike Harrison,
me, Bryson Graham.

It was significant for me that
we were on Island Records,
too. As far as I was concerned,
Island was Britain's version of
Atlantic, a proper, prestigious
record label with a range of
different bands that included
Free, Traffic, Nick Drake,
Fairport Convention, Roxy
Music, King Crimson, and a
reggae act who they had great
belief in, Bob Marley and the
Wailers. Like Atlantic, who had
a very charismatic founder and
figurehead in Ahmet Ertegun,
Island had Chris Blackwell. I
admired both men as record
people. Blackwell was very
pleasant to talk to, but also a
little mysterious and as such
his special qualities were
not so evident. It was only in
time that you found out just
how shrewd a businessman
he could be—in the end,
he managed to sell Spooky
Tooth to three different record
companies in America.

All Sewn Up

Our second album, *Witness*, was released
six months later that same year (1973),
and by then we had developed into a much
stronger and more cohesive unit. I co-
wrote what I thought was a really good
track, 'All Sewn Up' with Gary and we were
boosted considerably by the return of the
band's original drummer, Mike Kellie. As
a personality, Kellie could be quite difficult
to get along with, but there was a unique
and completely different feel about his style
of playing. There's a song titled 'Waitin'
for the Wind' on the band's second album,
Spooky Two, and to my mind the beginning
of that track was as significant in rock
as, say, Chic's 'Good Times' was in disco
and dance music. Kellie's opening drum
rhythm has a little bit of soul in there;
no-one in rock had quite played that way
before, but it soon became the basis of a
lot of well-known songs.

Being in Spooky Tooth allowed me to
witness up close what has since been
recognized as a great era for music. Led
Zeppelin had kick-started the rock (as
opposed to rock 'n' roll) movement that our
band was a part of, and were respected as
such by musicians. We had our own groove
going too, which was obviously a lot to do
with Kellie. He was a huge John Bonham
fan and the two of them had both come up
on the same club scene in Birmingham
and the English Black Country area. I had
to adapt my own style from what I'd been
playing in France, but the kind of music
I was listening to had changed, too. Gary
turned me on to quite a few soul artists

Original Spooky Tooth
drummer Mike Kellie.

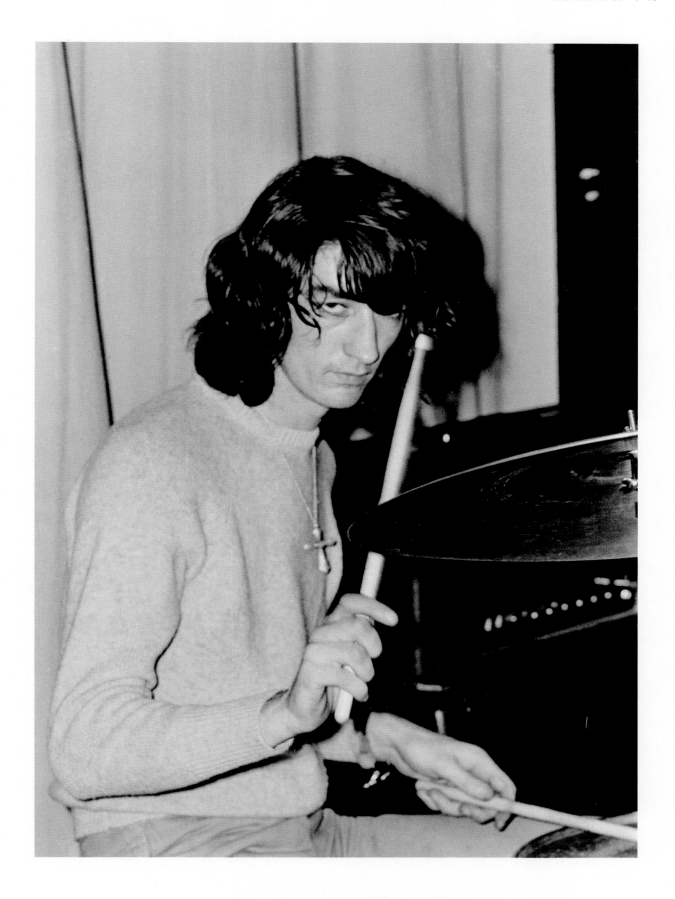

George Harrison in the
grounds of his gothic
mansion Friar Park,
around the time we
made *Dark Horse*.

who were recording at that time like Donny
Hathaway, and I was especially blown away by
Sly Stone's former bass player, Larry Graham,
who was fronting his own band, Graham Central
Station.

Because Gary had worked with George Harrison
quite a bit, and had included bassist Klaus
Voormann and drummer Alan White in his
Wonderwheel project before I joined, both of
whom were regular sidemen for the ex-Beatle,
he was always in contact with George. In
January, 1974, Gary traveled to India with George
to visit Ravi Shankar, and on their return began
to work on two albums. One was for a band
named Splinter who were the first act signed to
George's own record label Dark Horse, and the
other a new solo album for George, which was to
be titled *Dark Horse*.

I was very happy to be asked to put down an
acoustic guitar part on a song titled 'Ding Dong,
Ding Dong' for *Dark Horse*. Outside of Sylvie and
Johnny, the only major session gig I'd done up
till then had been to play on a track the previous
year for Peter Frampton's first solo record, *Wind
of Change*, but that had been a routine gig.

George, on the other hand, invited me down
to Friar Park, his Gothic mansion in Henley.
That was an amazing place, and had an almost
fantastical, fairy-tale setting. The former Beatles
PR man Derek Taylor called it, "a dream on a
hill," and it certainly didn't look like many places
I'd seen. The grounds were amazing, with a
grotto and a pond with stones just under the
surface so that you could look as if you were
walking on water as you crossed it. George had
his photo taken on the front lawn for the cover of
his 1970 solo album, *All Things Must Pass*, seated
among the gnomes which lived there.

Inside the house there was a minstrel's gallery
with alcoves and stained glass windows on the
first floor, which George used as part of his
home studio. He set both of us up in one of the
alcoves, cramped together with just a floor mic
to share. I distinctly remember using a Harptone
guitar for the recording because George had
turned me on to that model, he having played
one on 'My Sweet Lord.' That was a great day:
Gary Wright played piano on the track, Klaus
Voorman was on bass, and both Jim Keltner and
Ringo Starr played the drums. Then we all went
out to dinner together afterwards.

Fantasy Satisfier

OPPOSITE: Sunday on
Orchard Street in New York's
Lower East Side in 1976.
ABOVE: The Bronx was
burning and buildings were
falling down when I moved to
New York in the mid-1970s.

While Gary was in India with George, Spooky
Tooth singer Mike Harrison left the band, having
decided to go solo. He was replaced by Mike
Patto just at the point that we realized that
Spooky Tooth was getting a better reception
in the States than at home in Britain. After a
short period of consideration, it was decided
that we'd relocate to New York and concentrate
on the American market. Going off to live in the
Big Apple certainly appealed to me and I got an
apartment on the West Side of Manhattan, on
34th Street, right next to the Lincoln Tunnel. It
had a big cream shag carpet, as I recall, and I
was sharing the place with a friend of Gary's.
Unfortunately, this so-called friend ended
up making off with the money I was paying
him in rent rather than handing it over to the
landlord, and so I was evicted. That was when

I realized what a ruthless city New York could be—someone arrived one morning and stripped the apartment of everything, including anything that was ours. All that I was able to salvage were some clothes and a couple of guitars.

At the time New York looked and smelled like a war zone in parts. Huge blocks of the Bronx were collapsing, or being burned down. The city was officially bankrupt and bankers had called in their loans, which meant cuts to the city's services and it didn't take long for trash to pile up in the street as the bins went un-emptied.

Times Square was porno central, where it seemed that every building was a cinema under whose marquees drug dealers, prostitutes and their pimps paraded nightly—and many of them daily, too. The Lower East Side, which by 2016 had become one of the most expensive areas of real estate in Manhattan, was populated by squatting artists, junkies, and down-and-outs, the streets mostly empty day and night. Central Park was made up of a network of "muggers alleys," and at night it also boasted the best locations for buying rough sex (so I heard). Having no place to live in New York in the mid-

1970s was commonplace for many, but there were acres of unoccupied buildings slowly rotting away in different parts of Manhattan and the five boroughs and so few went without a roof of some sort over their head. Warehouses and brownstones with broken windows became squats in what would now be considered areas of choice real estate.

I was not in that dire a position, of course, and being temporarily homeless was soon enough the least of my worries. I found an apartment on the Upper West Side, at 91st and Riverside, and while it wasn't the Bronx it was still a cheap area because the neighborhood wasn't exactly cozy. For a good idea of what it was like, you can watch the movie *Death Wish* starring Charles Bronson, from 1974, because it was all filmed there. Initially I thought it would be fine; after all I'd grown up in London, and lived in Paris, both big cities with areas that were rough and tough.

Neither were New York—rough and tough though, and at times it was scary living there. More than once I was tailed by big cars with rolled-up windows, the occupants staring at me as I made my way quickly from the subway station to my apartment, and I never truly felt comfortable being on the streets around there after dark.

However, all through the summer of 1974 we made another album, *The Mirror*, with Eddie Kramer producing. Eddie was fresh from engineering Zeppelin's *Houses of the Holy* and we were on a roll, but even before the album was released, Gary announced that he was leaving the band and going solo again. His move came completely out of the blue and when he upped and quit the band to go back to his solo career, it left the rest of us high and dry in New York. He went back to New Jersey, got a new manager (Dee Anthony) who signed him to a deal with Warner Brothers Records, and set about

After he'd dropped Spooky Tooth, Gary had a solo hit with 'Dream Weaver' in 1976. It almost ruined my vacation.

recording a new album, using keyboards only, no guitar or bass.

Although the album didn't do too well when it came out in the middle of 1975, Gary had a big hit with the album title track, 'Dream Weaver' as a single in 1976, which then propelled the album into the charts that year. When the single hit, I was on vacation with my second wife Felicia, in the Florida Keys. We were staying at a poky little hotel that had a jukebox out by the swimming pool, and all I ever heard playing on it, day and night, was 'Dream Weaver'—until it got to the point where I totally lost it. I ran around the place screaming, "Will someone turn that bloody thing off!" It brought back to me what a shit Gary had been, and how he'd soured all my memories of being with Spooky Tooth. There was one good thing to come out of the episode, though, and that was it made my mind up that I was determined to do something in my musical career, "Wright," I told myself, "I'm going to show you." Not that I had a clue as to what my next move was going to be. I was 30 years old, and seriously considered returning to England and starting over a whole new career, such as going to medical school or becoming a dentist.

Goodear

Rather than look at other people's teeth for a living though, I accepted a job from Spooky Tooth's manager Nigel Thomas, to run a record label that he owned, called Goodear Records. It looked like a great deal for me. Nigel made me president of the label, gave me the chance to get back into producing, and we worked out of the Lieber and Stoller office in the famous old Brill Building on Broadway and 49th Street in New York. Plus, Nigel even threw a swanky apartment into the bargain which was closer to midtown than the *Death Wish* one. Unfortunately, though, Nigel was quite a bounder. He comported himself as an English gentleman and lovable rogue but actually, he had no morals whatsoever and ripped people off left, right, and center, including his artists. Since I had some musical credentials, Nigel used me to lure people to the label and we signed some talented artists. Spooky's former singer Mike Harrison cut a couple of singles for Goodear, for instance. And I produced a pretty good track with an American soul

Spooky Tooth manager and owner of Goodear Records Nigel Thomas getting paid in cash after a gig in 1972.

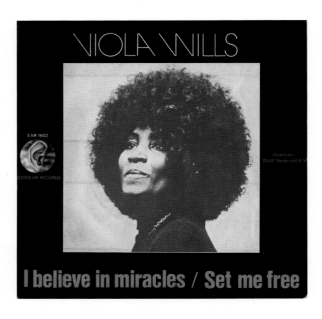

VIOLA WILLS

EAR 1602

I believe in miracles / Set me free

singer named Viola Wills, 'I Believe in Miracles,' which she'd written herself. Viola had been Joe Cocker's backing singer and Nigel had managed Joe for a while, which is how he knew her. Viola had six children before she was 21 and worked with Barry White, before Joe. Luckily for her and her children, she went on to have a big hit with a disco version of the 1950s song 'Gonna Get Along Without You' in 1979. But that wasn't for Goodear. At Goodear, we didn't manage to have any hits. Instead, I found myself getting into all sorts of tight spots with Nigel. He sent me off around the world to collect money from various deals he'd done with publishing companies, all of whom got shafted in the end. At one point, Nigel became determined to buy Stax Records, hook, line, and sinker, and to secure a loan for the deal, he arranged for us to have dinner one night with the president of the Union Planters Bank in Memphis. We finished our meal and Nigel handed over his credit card to pay the bill. Of course, it bounced. The *maitre d'* cut Nigel's card up, right in front of this guy we were trying to persuade to lend us millions of dollars. Even the deal he'd done on my apartment proved to be

dodgy. Felicia and I hadn't been living there more than a few days when we were evicted.

At the Brill Building though, I at least got to meet a couple of brothers, Johnny and Freddy Bienstock, who were reputable music publishers and owned the Elvis catalogue. Nigel did a number on them as well, but they didn't hold that against me (I guess that dealing with Elvis' manager, "Colonel" Tom Parker might have been far worse). In fact, I developed quite a rapport with Johnny and Freddy and when all the shit Nigel had stirred finally blew up in his face, they offered me a lifeline. On their behalf, they asked me if I wanted to open and run a studio in Nashville and form a production company. It was another good opportunity, but I'd grown uncomfortable being on the other side of the desk. I knew by then that I just wasn't cut out to be a corporate guy. Plus, I had found myself on the wrong end of a sniffy, kind of sneering attitude from some of the musicians I'd worked with for being a company man. I turned Johnny and Freddy down, but with no hard feelings on either side. Serendipitously though, very soon

Me in the studio, working
on my own songs for a
change, New York, 1976.

OPPOSITE: A promo copy
of a Leslie West Band EP.
BELOW: Mountain (L-R)
Felix Pappalardi, Corky
Laing, Leslie West.

after that a full-time band gig pretty much fell into my lap. Through working with Goodear, I'd been introduced to Bud Prager, the manager of guitarist Leslie West, whose band Mountain had not long before broken up, and he was looking for a second guitar player for West's solo band. Bud arranged for me to have an audition and Leslie loved the way I played, so offered me the role. The arrangement was a little odd for me because obviously Leslie was the focal point, and I was more or less being hired to be a back-up rhythm player. But Leslie was very warm and welcoming, so I decided it was worth a shot.

Ex-Mountain drummer, Corky Laing, was also in the band, and the three of us wrote a bunch of songs together and cut an album as the Leslie West Band. It was a good record, I thought, and we played some excellent shows. But then things quickly deteriorated. It's been well-documented that Leslie had a drug problem at the time and it was that which caused the band to break up. At one point he went into rehab and we thought

he was doing great; he was testing clean—but we soon discovered that he'd done a deal with a fellow patient whereby they swapped each other's urine every day. One of the last shows we did together was in New York. Towards the end of our set, Leslie walked off stage and simply disappeared. It turned out that he had taken his guitar down to a store on 48th Street and pawned it to buy drugs. I lit into Bud after that, because I thought that Leslie was being enabled to get away with that kind of behavior, and quit the band that night. However, I could see that Bud was a bright guy, so I told him I was going to form a band myself and if he wanted to, he could become my manager. The two of us argued back and forth for a week or so, until Bud finally accepted my challenge. He had to borrow $100,000 from his wife's trust fund to finance the deal (paying for equipment and rehearsal space, etc.) and I don't think she knew a thing about it until years afterwards, but from that moment on, Bud and I formed a close bond.

Foreigner

When Mountain split up, Bud's business partner, Gary Kurfirst, took to managing the other creative half of the band, Felix Pappalardi. In the late 1960s, Felix had become known for producing Cream's *Disraeli Gears*, and along with his wife Gail Collins, co-wrote 'Strange Brew' with Eric Clapton. He founded Mountain with Leslie, played bass, sang, and co-wrote a lot of the material, with Gail and Leslie. Leslie later said the band split because Gail wanted to be the power in the group, and maybe that was the

case. In any event, she ended up shooting Felix dead in 1983, and served time for a criminally negligent act of homicide. However, in 1976 I benefited from Felix's having built a small studio in the offices of Bud and Gary, and used it as a writing room to begin with, later auditioning and rehearsing the band. That studio was a life-saver for me, because at the time I had to get by on $100 a week. I wrote four songs quite quickly, one of which was 'Feels Like the First Time.' They sounded interesting and decent enough to

me, and I felt a surge of excitement, as if I had been released from a confinement of sorts.

While writing songs, I got to know a guy called Ian Lloyd. We started hanging out together quite a lot, throwing a baseball around or going for a run in Central Park. It was only after we'd formed a friendship that I discovered Ian had been the original front man with a New York band called the Stories, who three years earlier had a Number One hit with a cover of

OPPOSITE: The first Foreiger lineup, posed for Atlantic Records in 1976, (L-R) Al Greenwood, Ian McDonald, Dennis Elliott, me, Ed Gagliardi, Lou Gramm.
RIGHT: Ian Lloyd, the voice on the Foreigner demos.

American Al Greenwood,
my first keyboard-playing
recruit.

the Hot Chocolate song, 'Brother Louie' and
then recorded an album with Eddie Kramer
producing, titled *About Us*. 'Louie' had ended up
being something of a millstone around Ian's neck
though, because he was in fact a fan of harder,
progressive rock bands like Genesis and King
Crimson, and had a great, raspy sort of voice.
But he was pigeon-holed after the hit single,
and when we met he was stuck out on what they
called the chitlin' circuit, playing poky soul joints.

Ian was a wonderful guy. Not only did he help
me to settle into New York life, but he sang guide
vocals on the initial tracks I'd written and put me
in touch with some of his contacts. I'd already
found a keyboard player, Al Greenwood, but Ian
had become friendly with another Englishman
who played keys among other instruments,
Ian McDonald, who worked on his solo debut
album (*Ian Lloyd*, 1976). Ian Mac had played
guitar, keyboards, and flute in King Crimson
and was just then doing some session work in
New York, so I asked him to come by Bud and
Gary's little studio for a jam. King Crimson was
a big deal at the time, and I had a great regard
for Ian's playing. All along I had pictured there
being a multi-instrumentalist in my band and he
was perfect for that role, since he was the kind
of intuitive musician who could add different
textures and colors to any song.

Dennis Elliott came in soon after Ian. We met
when I was doing some session work with Ian
Hunter in upstate New York. Dennis was Ian's
drummer and I was immediately impressed with
him, so over the next couple of months I subtly
tried to tempt him away from Ian. Finally, he
succumbed and became a huge, integral part of
the band's sound. Dennis isn't a flashy player,

he's slightly understated if anything, but he has
an acute sense of feel and real power. Right from
the start, Dennis and I locked in so well together
that we didn't need to hear a bass part. That was
perhaps why bassist Ed Gagliardi was the last
of the musicians to come into the fold. By then I
had a name for the band, too, which was Trigger.
However, there was still no singer. Although
Ian had sung all the vocal parts on the demos, I
just couldn't fit him into the set up. My aim was
not to make the band a super-group, but to try
and discover new, raw talent, and especially so
in the case of our singer. We auditioned at least
40 candidates, but without success. It got to the

point where I was tempted to give the job to Ian , and it was a very close-run thing, but Ian's voice just wasn't quite right for the overall sound that I had in my head.

After I'd spent at least six months searching in vain for a singer, I was almost tearing my hair out in frustration. One afternoon, I was up in the studio finishing off the backing track for the demo of 'Feels Like the First Time.' On the mixing desk, there was a big stack of records that I'd been sent. Just for a break and to take my mind off the task at hand, I pulled out from the pile a Black Sheep album, *Encouraging*

OPPOSITE: From King Crimson to Foreigner: multi-instrumentalist and founder member, Briton Ian McDonald.
ABOVE: Foreigner's original drummer in action, Briton Dennis Elliott.

Words, which my old label friend had mailed to me. Within ten seconds of putting it on the turntable, I knew that I had found *the* voice. I had previously met Lou Gramm when I was on tour in the US with Spooky Tooth. Our East Coast promotion guy at the time lived upstate in Rochester and in his spare time was managing Lou's band, Black Sheep. He brought Lou along to one of our shows, and we chatted backstage that night, about nothing specific. But he was playing drums at the time and figured that was going to be his ultimate destiny. Hearing the Black Sheep album though, I had to disagree with him.

Having heard that Black Sheep album I set about tracking Lou down, which I managed to do quickly; he was in Rochester, working on a building site. When I called the number I had been given for him, he was halfway up a ladder carrying bricks, but he came down to take the call. He told me that he'd kind of stopped singing, was fed up with it, and was concentrating on the drums. I was astonished, because he clearly had a fantastic voice, and I knew it had the potential to put him right up there in the hierarchy of classic rock singers. Anyway, we chatted and eventually I persuaded him to come down to New York for a few days. 'Long, Long Way From Home' on our debut album was written about that conversation and what followed. As Lou wrote in the first line of the song, it really *was* a Monday when I called.

The first day that Lou joined us in New York, we ran through a couple of songs with him, and it was like being hit by a bolt of lightning. I knew right away that this could be the start of something special. Lou had a feel for soul music, which was a great credential in my book, and then again he had a certain indefinable magic. He hadn't, though, ever worked

Our first bassist, left-handed American Ed Gagliardi.

with anybody who could help him to shape his voice—with the phrasing, the key, and on melodies—in the way that I would be able to do.

With Lou on board, we completed our demo tape and had it sent to Jerry Moss at A&M. Jerry was another of the great record men of that era; he and his partner Herb Albert had signed Humble Pie, Free, Procul Harum, and Joe Cocker to their label in America, which, for me, made A&M a good home for us. However, I found out later that Jerry had gone on holiday the very morning our tape arrived, and so didn't hear it. That was always a big regret for me. The tape also went out to Atlantic and was returned to us. The head of A&R there had discarded it without even taking it out of the box. Bud, though, had connections at Atlantic and soon made headway in getting it listened to, which was when John Kalodner arrived on the scene.

When I heard the Black Sheep album, I knew that American Lou Gramm was the voice Foreigner needed. He proved it in his first studio session with us, in 1976.

Feels Like the First Time

(Mick Jones)

I wrote this song right after the Leslie West Band had broken up. That had been a crazy period of my life, which I survived and then had to go back to trying to scrape a living in New York. One day, I started to mess around on the guitar and alighted on the chord structure that subsequently became the main riff. It's probably one of the band's most instantly recognizable tracks, but came to me so instinctively that it really did feel as if it were the first time I had written a song. Certainly, it was the first time in a good while that I had been quite so engaged in what I was doing. The lyrics speak for themselves. It's not a profound or deep lyric by any means, but just then it fit my mood. After several years where it seemed to me as if I were stuck in a long, dark tunnel, I could finally see a chink of light again.

RELEASED
March 1977, c/w
'Woman, Oh Woman'
(Jones)

PRODUCED
Gary Lyons, John
Sinclair

Foreigner fun in the sun and
snow, (L-R) Dennis, me, Ian,
Ed, Al, Lou, February 1977.

Inside Looking Outside

John Kalodner would go on to sign both Peter Gabriel and Phil Collins to Atlantic, and to have great success at Geffen and Columbia record labels, but right then he was the new kid at Atlantic, and prior to joining the label he had been working as a rock journalist. When he looked at the line-up of the band he knew about me, Ian, and to a certain extent Dennis, and so wanted to hear our tape. He thought it was fantastic and from that point on caused pandemonium at Atlantic, pestering everyone at the label to listen to our demo, yelling and screaming at people. In fact, he became a right royal pain in the ass on our behalf—but he got us heard. The tape finally made its way up to Atlantic's president, Jerry Greenberg, and a few weeks after that, John brought Jerry down to our studio. Within a few days of that visit, we had been signed to Atlantic. I never forgot that time I'd watched the red and black label on the Ray Charles record going around and around on a turntable, almost as if it was sending a message to me. I'd heard it and now my dream of being a part of that musical legend had come true. It was John who, not unwisely, suggested we ditch Trigger as our band name. That was when I came up with Foreigner, to reflect the make-up of the group, being three Brits and three

Americans. Since we had three rookies in the band, I felt I had to lead the way in all respects and very much took the reins from the moment that we were signed. Indeed, it was that time when I truly realized just how much of a control freak I am.

Discussions began immediately about making a record, and I wanted to work with Roy Thomas Baker on our first album. Roy had worked with Free and Ian Hunter, but had made his name by producing Queen. Unfortunately, though, he was booked to work on Ian Hunter's *Overnight Angels* album. However, he did recommend Gary Lyons to me because he had engineered all the Queen stuff for him. Gary in turn wanted to bring along a co-producer with him, another English guy named John Sinclair, who happened to be Trevor Horn's brother-in-law.

The pair of them came over to New York to meet with me and we all seemed to be on the same page. I was particularly interested in getting an instantly recognizable vocal sound and of certain songs using background vocal choruses. We had a couple of days' trial in our studio and I was immediately impressed with the drum sound that Gary got. He clearly knew what he was doing and was very enthusiastic, so took a chance and gave it a go; he had the job. It was the first project that either Gary or John had produced on their own, although I was their co-producer. Ian McDonald also put in a tremendous amount of work, and he was great on technical details of sound. The songs came together quite quickly, and because I knew Lou had been a writer in his previous bands I encouraged him right from the word go. I thought that it was important that if he was going to be singing the songs that he had some input to them, so he could express them properly on the record. If he was involved in them personally as well in the writing stage, he would be able to express the real feeling of the songs. Lou began to share in the songwriting, and we gelled very quickly. From then on we gradually built our partnership and writing relationship. There was no real method to the way we worked. He would come up with an idea or I would come up with an idea, and we'd throw it back and forth

and see what it did for us, and then if we had something that sounded like it had potential, we'd focus in on it and try and finish the number. We never sat down and tried to construct hits—the main focus for me was simply to try and make good albums. Obviously, they had to have some appeal commercially, but I was an album kind of guy.

For me what counted was being able to make an album that people could listen to from the top to the bottom with no fillers. But we were never consciously putting anything tacky in there, it was all pretty natural and from the heart. There was no 'formula' as such—the only formula is the sound of the guitar and the vocal, really. That's the only thing that obviously goes through every song. We recorded the album at the Atlantic Studios on Broadway and 60th in New York (which sadly closed in 1991), and then Gary and John took it off to London to do the mix. I still didn't have a green card though, and couldn't leave

Wish I still had that suit...

America in case they wouldn't let me back in, so Ian had to accompany them on our behalf. The idea was that he would oversee the mix, but the first time I called him at the studio, it was obvious all was not well. I asked how it was going and he replied, "Um... I can't say right now." They FedEx-ed a couple of the mixes to me the next day and while they were interesting, the tracks sounded miles away from what I had envisioned for the band. I had all of the master tapes sent back to me in New York where Ian and I, along with a staff engineer at Atlantic named Jimmy Douglass, set about remixing the album in a very short period of time.

By then, we were already running a month over our deadline and racking up costs. I didn't know it then, but that would become the norm for us, but I was determined that the record sound representative of the band as I wanted them to sound. After a month of mastering, I finally felt able to take the completed master tape home with me. I put it on that night, and played it pretty loudly. I'd had a little smoke, and I was laid out on the floor, staring up at the ceiling.

That was one of the most glorious moments of my life.

OPPOSITE: The promotional photo used in all our first album publicity, (L-R) Lou, Ed, Ian, Al, me and Dennis.
ABOVE: The debut album's artwork had us all packed, wearing very fashionable trenchcoats and ready to travel. I think that's me in the green coat.

It's Where They're Going

While I genuinely believed the record was good enough for us to start making a name for ourselves, no one in their right mind could have predicted what it would go on to become.

In any event, the kind of success that we went on to have was near enough unprecedented. The only new band to have done anything like it was Boston, whose debut album released the previous year had been a phenomenon. Almost nobody else up to that point, including the Stones or Zeppelin, had sold a million records straight off. The *Foreigner* album passed that mark in just weeks. I can only put that down to how strong the songs were, since we didn't have a particular image, or a gimmick to trade on. We were only the second band on Atlantic to go platinum, after Iron Butterfly. But their *In-A-Gadda-Da-Vida* album (of 1968) had taken eight years to do it, whereas we raced on to two, three and then five million sales within a year or so. Truly, the only two bands that were up there with us that year were Fleetwood Mac with *Rumours* and the Eagles with *Hotel California*.

My mind has retained only snapshots from that time, since the whole thing was a blur to me. I remember us heading up to Chicago to do our first radio session. We played the album front to back for a handful of people in the station studio, just as the buzz on it was really beginning to grow. Early on, we also did a bunch of shows as the opening act for Uriah Heep, with Ted Nugent also on the bill. There were then a string of dates supporting the Doobie Brothers, which helped to bring us to the attention of a wider audience.

As the album took off, we began to play some shows of our own. Going out as the headline act for the first time is a testing experience, the kind of thing that separates the men from the boys. Quite often we had AC/DC who were also signed to Atlantic, as our opening act and a faction at the label was desperate to have them break America. They were an especially tough act to have to follow, as were Cheap Trick who also opened for us on our first US arena tour. Their guitarist Rick Nielsen and I became pals on that trip. Cheap Trick were determined to throw down a live challenge to us, and they would go out

Me, Dennis and Ed
rocking out at what
was Ed's first live
Foreigner show.

every night and try to blow us off the stage. But
we held our own, I think.

I enjoyed the whole experience completely, and
massively, but it was hard to comprehend. I was
the most experienced member of the band, but
nothing—not even Johnny Hallyday-style French
stardom—can prepare anyone for that kind of
whirlwind success. That said, I don't think at
the outset that it changed the band too much,
because no-one was easily impressed. I mean,
a couple of the guys went out and bought stuff,
put down payments on cars for instance, but in
general what all of us felt more than anything
was an overwhelming sense of pride at what we
had accomplished. It was also important to me
that we sustain, and built on what the album
had done for us, and I didn't waste any time in

OPPOSITE: The crucifix
was pure decoration.
ABOVE: Foreigner
receiving a gold record
for the *Foreigner* LP
in Australia. L-R: Bud
Prager, Dennis Elliott,
Al Greenwood, me,
Phil Carson
(Senior Vice-President,
Atlantic Records),
Ed Gagliardi, Lou
Gramm, John Kalodner
(Vice-President A&R,
Atlantic Records), Ian
McDonald.

getting down to writing new songs with Lou.
Two of them, 'Hot Blooded' and 'Double Vision,'
even made their way into our live set before we'd
finished touring the *Foreigner* album. In fact, I
think we played each of them for the first time
at the California Jam II in March 1978, and in
front of 200,000 people, too. That was an almost
surreal experience, not least because when
you're looking out at a crowd that big you can
see a curvature; it tapers off at the corners and
forms an arc. That's really a wild thing to see
from the stage.

Highlights from the show which also featured
Aerosmith, Heart, and Santana, were broadcast
on the ABC network to an audience of several
million, too, so opening us up to an even bigger
potential audience.

Cold as Ice

(Lou Gramm, Mick Jones)

This was one of the first songs that I ever wrote on the piano. I had been listening to Queen a lot at the time, and while it wasn't stolen from them, it definitely bears their influence. When we recorded it for Foreigner's debut album at the Atlantic studios in New York, I got to play the exact same piano that Aretha Franklin had used on a bunch of her classic hits in the late-'60s. Let me tell you, there sure was some soul in that piano. Funnily enough, Billy Joel used to play 'Cold as Ice' with his band but in a different key. When I worked with him on his *Storm Front* album, I made sure to show him how to do it the right way.

RELEASED
July 1977 c/w 'I Need You'

PRODUCED
Gary Lyons, John Sinclair

Lou and me rocking out on stage—we made a great team.

I will never forget the first time we played at one of Bill Graham's famous Day on the Green shows at Oakland Coliseum. That was May 28th 1977, and we were opening on a bill that also included Heart, the Steve Miller Band, and the Eagles, who were headlining.

There was something like 80,000 people in the audience, and Bill invited me up onto the stage just before the stadium gates were opened, because he said he wanted to show me something. It was a daytime festival, so this was around 8.30 a.m. We stood there for

a few minutes, just looking out at the space in front of the stage when all of a sudden, people began to run from out of black holes in the stands, looking like scurrying mice. It is simply mind-blowing to see that amount of bodies gather together in one place.

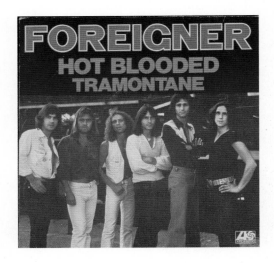

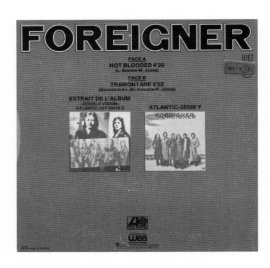

Double Vision

A young Mutt Lange lobbied to produce our second album. He was only just starting to make a name for himself, having worked with Graham Parker and the Boomtown Rats most recently, and I was initially interested in the idea. But once we met, it seemed to me as though he was going through something in his life at the time and wasn't the best fit with what we wanted to do. So our relationship was postponed (I thought we'd work together at some point in the future, even then) and we went instead with Keith Olsen, who had produced Fleetwood Mac's first album with Stevie Nicks and Lindsey Buckingham, *Fleetwood Mac* (the one with 'Rhiannon' on it). In fact, it was Keith who introduced Buckingham and Nicks to Mick Fleetwood, because the pair had been living with him when he produced their *Buckingham Nicks* album in 1973.

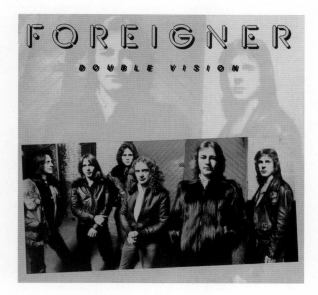

OPPOSITE; A French single sleeve—Foreigner were a hit everywhere, almost immediately.
RIGHT: The second album cover (top) and front cover of a Greek music mag, 1978.

With Keith on board as producer and engineer, we recorded *Double Vision* at Atlantic Studios once more, but on this occasion my overriding impression was that we weren't getting a sound that was hard-edged enough. Nevertheless, no sooner had we finished the basic tracks, at the beginning of 1978 than we had the crazy idea of doing a rapid, high-speed tour of the world. Off we went, and I got Keith to FedEx mixes out to wherever we happened to be. I got an average of two a day from him and some sounded OK, but others didn't.

Yet again, Ian, Jimmy Douglass, and I had to scramble back into the studio and go through the same arduous procedure as we had on the first record, in order to get the mix I wanted.

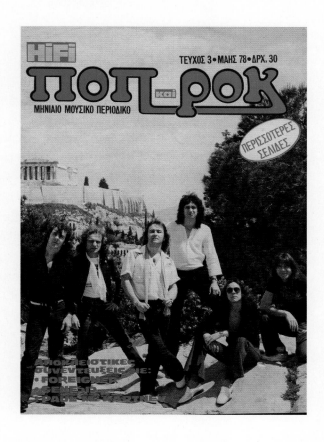

Hot Blooded

(Lou Gramm, Mick Jones)

I wanted us to have a very strong, hard rocking opening track for the *Double Vision* album as a kind of statement of intent. This song was actually written entirely in the studio, and as a result of us just jamming around. Dennis Elliott and I fell in to a certain rhythm together and once we had started our playing became more and more intense. All of a sudden, I smelled burning. I turned around and there was smoke coming out from my amp. Right then I thought to myself that we had to get "hot" into the title of the song. Not long after the album came out, I got a call one night from Ted Nugent. He told me: "Mick, there are cats around would chew your old boots off to play a solo like that one on 'Hot Blooded'." Ted's crazy, but a great guitar player, and that was a cool compliment.

RELEASED
June 1978 c/w
'Tramontane'

PRODUCED
Mick Jones, Keith
Olsen

This, though, if anything was even more painstaking than it had been on the first album, and I agonized over every note and detail. But I believe you can hear the value of that in the finished result. In the end, we fashioned our own sound, or maybe it would be more accurate to describe it as my sound, on *Double Vision*. It would also be true to say that I was very hard to please, but by then I had learned a valuable lesson; a producer could be very helpful if they really knew about arrangements and song structure. However, if they were nothing more than a glorified engineer, then it was obvious that I would be better off managing the mixing of our records myself.

Still, we escaped what they call the sophomore jinx with *Double Vision*. It ended up selling even more than the first record—the last I heard it was up to ten million copies with seven million of that number sold in America. That would be an unimaginable amount 40 years later, with the state of the record business being such that people no longer buy albums, but download or stream them instead. I sometimes feel desperately sorry that people stopped getting the same thrill from the whole album experience. Those were magical times and the album was

perceived as a true work of art. Indeed, very often the LP covers were more interesting than the actual music.

Again, specific moments stand out for me from the tour we did for *Double Vision*. Just as the album was about to come out that June of 1978, we did a show with the Rolling Stones at the JFK Stadium in Philadelphia. The Stones had just released their *Some Girls* album and there were 90,000 people present. Pete Tosh opened the show. We went on right before the Stones and to a roaring success. It's funny, but that was supposed to be the Stones' "farewell" tour, but obviously it wasn't and maybe that was because it was the first American tour on which Ronnie Wood was a proper member. He and Keith had such a good time on it that Keith went out on Ronnie's solo US tour the following year. According to some people, it was the guitarists who persuaded Mick to go out with the Stones again in 1981, after which they never stopped, of course.

We also got to headline at Madison Square Garden for the first time, which was one of those occasions when I could stand back and take stock of what was happening. For me at least, it

A record signing (I don't think they happen much any more). We were treated like bona fide pop stars!

was like reaching a summit after a long climb.

While we were still recording the album, I had happened to catch the Orson Welles movie, *Touch of Evil*, and had been very impressed by his use of light and shadow. That gave me the idea of doing something similar for our live shows. That culminated in us having these huge louvre windows constructed and hung on either side of the stage with banks of lights working behind them. When you start getting involved with lighting and stage engineers though, that's when the whole business ratchets up by hundreds of thousands of dollars in costs, of course. But there's also an intoxicating feeling of great power. I suppose we did begin to feel indestructible. Surviving Cheap Trick's onslaught had toughened us

By early 1978 we had proper rock star stage clothes and were really rocking. (L-R) me, Lou, Ed.

Dirty White Boy

(Lou Gramm, Mick Jones)

By the time we started work on the *Head Games* album, I was living the life of a rock star out in Los Angeles. Things got a little fuzzy for me for a while there and I was being unproductive, so I decided to go back to England for a change of pace and to get my head together. No sooner had I settled down in London than 'Dirty White Boy' popped into my head, almost fully formed. It was as if I had plucked it out of the ether. That was one of those moments as a musician when you really do feel as if you're channeling a higher power. What I was listening to at the time would also have made an impression. I can't recall precisely what it was, but it would have been interesting or curious to say the least, because for a good amount of the time I spent in England I would have the radio tuned in to the John Peel Show.

RELEASED
August 1979 c/w 'Rev on the Red Line'

PRODUCED
Roy Thomas Baker, Mick Jones, Ian McDonald

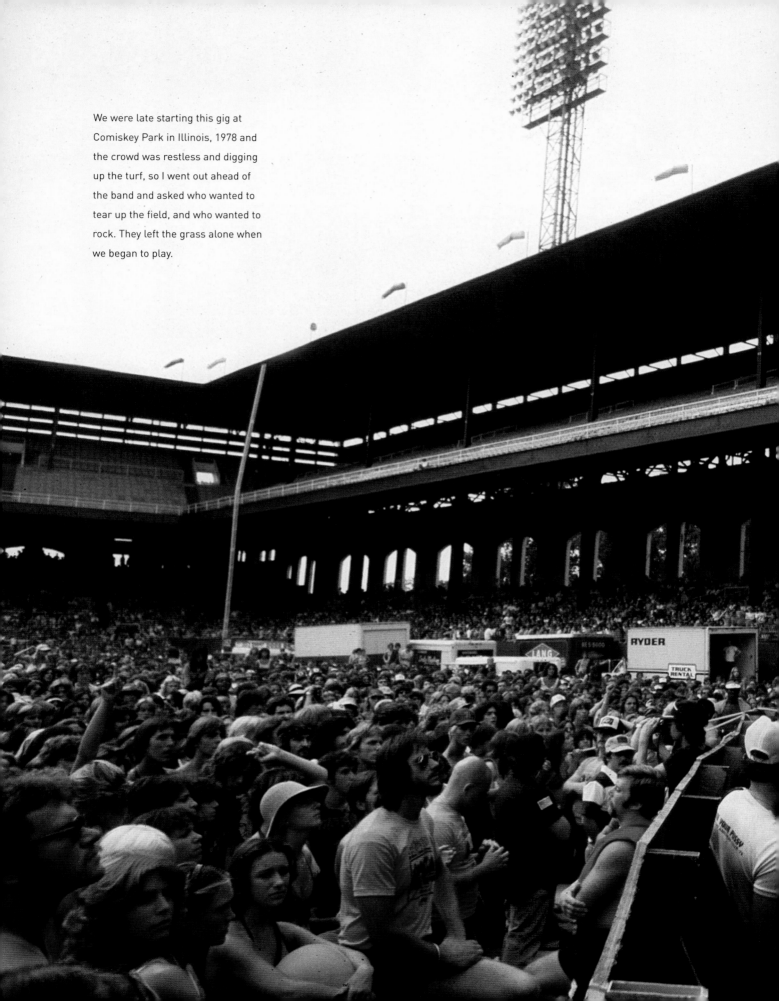

We were late starting this gig at
Comiskey Park in Illinois, 1978 and
the crowd was restless and digging
up the turf, so I went out ahead of
the band and asked who wanted to
tear up the field, and who wanted to
rock. They left the grass alone when
we began to play.

Our third album, which wasn't
as successful as the previous
two: some people blamed
the cover artwork, but I don't
think that's fair.

up, and I think we came across as not having any
bullshit about us. We were down to earth, not
showy, and our audience was better able to relate
to the band. In short, what we perhaps projected
most of all was that there didn't appear to be any
assholes in Foreigner.

Head Games

Every band is vulnerable in the face of huge
success though, and it transpired that we
were no exception. There had been a little bit
of difficulty with the communication between
Dennis Elliott and Ed Gagliardi for a while, and a
few months earlier when Rick Wills was coming
through New York he'd rung me. He came down
to the studio and we didn't talk specifically about
him joining the band, but we did stay in touch,
and one day a few weeks after, Dennis asked if
Rick could come down and maybe jam with the
band—so he did.

It was immediately obvious to me that this was
the sort of the rhythm section that we had been

searching for, and it was really so good that there was no question that we had to make a change. Because basically I played bass on the first two albums for maybe 90 percent of the tracks, I needed someone to come and relieve me of that duty. While I enjoy playing bass, I tend to keep it simple but I felt it was important to have a real understanding between the rhythm section members. Rick had great pedigree, having played with David Gilmour in Cambridge before Pink Floyd had formed (and much later played on David's debut solo album, too). He played on the first three Peter Frampton albums, and then joined Roxy Music in 1976, before very briefly replacing Ronnie Lane in the mid-70s era Small Faces. With him on board we started work on the *Head Games* album. However, it proved to be a crazy and not especially constructive period for the band.

It began when we decided that we'd make *Head Games* in Los Angeles, and moved our base of operations to California. There must be something in the air of LA that adversely affects musicians (apart from the smog, that is), because once we were out on the West Coast

we started to live the life of rock stars. Quite simply, all the acclaim we were getting went to our heads a little bit. Almost from the moment of arrival, there was an awful lot of swanning around in Beverley Hills, partying and indulging in general "rock star" madness. It wasn't just us, though. The city was an odd and not altogether safe place to be back then. One afternoon Ian McDonald was mugged in his car, as he sat at a traffic light. Mind you, he was driving something as ostentatious as Johnny Hallyday's old open-topped Bentley.

One bonus of being there though, was that we at last got to work with Roy Thomas Baker. He was eccentric, jovial, had a very cynical sense of humor and knew his stuff inside-out. A Brit, he had come up in the business as an engineer, working at Decca Records in London from the age of 14. He moved to Trident Studios to work with Gus Dudgeon (who'd produced everybody and everything in the 1960s and '70s, including Bowie's 'Space Oddity' of 1969) and got to engineer for Frank Zappa, the Stones, and lots of other bands of that era, before becoming Queen's producer of choice. By the time we got

Ed and I had a great onstage
chemistry.

to work with him, Roy certainly had that something extra which separates real producers from mere studio hands. In the interim since our first album, Roy had made a couple of great records with Journey and the Cars, who had opened for us on a couple of dates during the *Double Vision* tour (and who would open for us on the *Foreigner 4* tour). I loved that band and had a great deal of admiration for their main songwriter, Ric Ocasek. He was a bit of a visionary, but a producer as well as songwriter, guitarist, and band leader—so we had that in common, at least.

Even when it came to someone as accomplished as Roy though, I found it hard to be produced. In some ways, I was way too much of a perfectionist when it came to work. There were times when I should have left things to be a little more raw-sounding, I know, and my approach could certainly piss people off—even though I always tried to let them down gently. With *Head Games* I wanted to make a record with a slightly more abrasive sound than we'd had on our two previous albums. I worked hard to get it, but was never sure that we had entirely captured the sound I wanted, and because of that grew increasingly frustrated

with the process of making it. That remains a record about which I have mixed feelings.

There is a general perception, I think, that we rushed the record out, but in fact the opposite was true. It was the first time that we'd recorded using 64 tracks and I was like a kid in a playground with the studio, able to try out all these different tape machines and mess around syncing them together. The drawback to that was that there was a lot of technical downtime, which only encouraged us to adopt a different kind of lifestyle.

At the time of its release, *Head Games* was viewed as something of a disappointment and it did prove to be a less commercial record than its predecessors. Lou came to be of the opinion that our sales were harmed because of the album's cover artwork. Personally, I'm not sure that was the case, but it's true that it caused us problems. The cover was the idea of a woman in the Atlantic art department named Sandi Young. She was a friend of a friend and out of curiosity we gave her the record to see what she would come up with. That photograph of the young girl in a men's restroom was the result. I wasn't involved in the process really, but thought it was a striking image. The trouble was, that back then if you stepped over a certain line, the people who lived in the great Bible Belt of America would turn against you.

In any event, by the time we finished touring *Head Games* I had other, and more pressing, things on my mind. I felt exhausted, and dissatisfied. I felt that there had been too much indulgence in every respect and not enough productivity. My reaction to that ultimately left us with just four people in Foreigner.

Lou, Dennis, Ian, Al, and I had been through a lot together. When we'd been thrust into the public eye we'd rallied around like family, but by the end of the *Head Games* tour cracks had begun to show in the foundations of Foreigner. It's difficult to pin-point one thing that pushed that line-up over the brink, but in general I felt we were losing focus and that divisions had begun

to grow. Ian wanted to concentrate more on the guitar and I think both he and Al felt they should have a greater input into the song-writing, which Lou and I had monopolized up to that point. For instance, there was a lovely little song called 'Zalia' that Lou and Ian wrote while we were making *Head Games*, and I really liked it, because it represented what I wanted to do from the very beginning, not just be a hard-rock band. I wanted the band to be able to rock, but I also wanted it to be able to show off some of the other talents in the band that might go a bit deeper melodically. 'Zalia,' was a great touch and a very different sounding song than anything we'd done at that point. It's one of those things that added a little different dimension, and we always sought to do that—certainly throughout those first four albums. Unfortunately, though, it didn't make the cut on the original release (although it did get on to a CD reissue, in 2002).

We were, though, doing our growing up in public. Because we'd set the bar so high on our first album, we were under tremendous pressure to deliver a massively successful record each time.

Essentially, I thought we'd reached an impasse as a unit and were unable to move on, so I called a meeting with Lou, Dennis, and Rick. I chatted about the situation with them and they seemed to feel the same way as I did, so the decision was made to part company with Ian and Al. Those situations are never easy to resolve and just as it had been with Ed, this one involved a difficult and tortuous process. In hindsight, I'm not sure if that was the right or wrong thing to have done, and it was certainly cold.

Bassist Rick Wills (left) on stage with Steve Marriott in the last incarnation of the Small Faces, just before he joined us.

Urgent

(Mick Jones)

I was living in upstate New York at the time. One afternoon I was at home, it was a beautiful day and I was sitting in the living room. I had a little cassette player that I used to put ideas down on and the hook to the song just started playing in my head, over and over. It obviously had a bit of a street, urban vibe to it, some funk going on, and I could already hear a slap bass on it. I wrote the entire lyrics in a couple of hours, top to bottom. When you get that kind of flow going and it's fresh, you just have to ride it.

When it came to recording it for *Foreigner 4*, we were taking a break one evening in the studio, and I picked up a copy of the *Village Voice*. I was absently flicking through it, checking out who was in town and thinking I might go and see someone or other

RELEASED
June 1981 c/w 'Girl on the Moon'

PRODUCED
Mick Jones,
Mutt Lange

play. The instrumental track we had cut for 'Urgent' was playing softly in the background and we had left a space for a solo. In the paper, I spotted an ad for a show by the great saxophonist Junior Walker and put two and two together. 'Urgent' seemed to me like it had the feel of one of those great R&B sides, like 'Roadrunner,' that Junior had cut in the '60s.

That night, I went down to the club he was playing and sat through three sets waiting to speak with him. Eventually, Junior's son, who played drums in his band, recognized me and fetched his father for me. Junior wandered over to my table and said, "I hear there's someone round here wants to make a record."

The thing was, though, with all the stuff that he had done at Motown, Junior had never once overdubbed onto a track. That was the first little hurdle Mutt Lange and I had to overcome; getting him comfortable.

But once he was ready and comfortable, he went over to the mic, pulled up a chair, sat down like a jazz player, and did a few passes playing in this sort of lounge style and without any of his trademark high notes and squeaks. This, he informed us, was his new style. I had to tell him with all due respect that his new style was not what we wanted. We had to coax him gently, but over the next few takes he gradually relented.

Mutt and I then spent two entire nights dedicated to editing Junior's solo together from the three or four tracks he eventually laid down. Each of them was great, but not all the way through, so we had to chop and change. The solo you hear on the record was made up of something ridiculous like 20 different snippets.

Afterwards, I asked our touring sax player at the time, Mark Rivera, if it would be humanly possible to play the part that we had created. He told me that it was, but only just about.

Junior actually got up and played the song with us at five arena shows on the American tour we did to promote *Foreigner 4*. I would guess he had only heard the song once or twice beforehand, but every night he came out and played that solo note for note, perfectly. That was a stunning thing to witness, but he was convinced that was the way that he had put it down on the record—in just the one take.

Fame + 4 Tunes

The pressure on us was made almost unbearable by the dip in sales we'd suffered with *Head Games*, but I went into the next record like a man on a mission. I wanted to show more dimensions of the band, and to create the complete album. On this occasion, Mutt Lange, who'd had enormous success with AC/DC's *Highway to Hell* (1979) and *Back to Black* (1980) albums since we last met, was available and ready to help me to realize my aim. Indeed, he came over to New York to be interviewed for the job and was obviously really on the ball. Up till then, the only work of Mutt's I'd heard was the first album he had done with an English band, City Boy, back in 1976, and I had thought there was something very appealing about that record.

One of Mutt's great strengths was that he had come up in radio in South Africa, where he was raised. He had started out singing jingles, because if you were a musician in South Africa at the time, that was your only hope of getting out of the country. Possibly because of that background Mutt had a very acute pop sensibility, which he combined with a flair for short, sharp choruses, and an understanding of the discipline of being in a studio. He was pretty hip to equipment, and was pushy, challenging and absolutely relentless.

Like me, Mutt's a spiritual guy, but very focused and serious, too. The two of us are quite strong-willed personalities and Mutt didn't mind

upsetting me, but we managed to work well, and constructively, despite what might have been a difficult situation. That was one of the real pluses of making *Foreigner 4* because, believe me, it could very easily have gone completely the other way. There were dodgy moments in the making of that record, occasions when Mutt and I would literally face off in the studio, but he wanted to prove himself and to make a statement—and ultimately, he was the guy who got the most out of the band by far.

We did clash though, and our first big bust-up was over the drums. We were working in New York at the Record Plant on West 44th Street, and on the third or fourth day of the sessions Mutt came in with electronic drums that he wanted to us to use. He ended up putting them on Def Leppard's albums, but I didn't want any part of that on our album. I wanted real drums, but Mutt insisted to me than Dennis didn't have perfect timing.

In those days, we weren't really stuck on having a fixed tempo all the way through a song. One of the things missing most today I think, with such things as click tracks and other technology used in making recorded music, is a sense of spontaneity and looseness. I told Mutt, "Dennis has nearly perfect timing, he can play perfectly if he wants to, and I'll prove it to you." I took Dennis into the main room and together the two of us ran through 'Break It Up'—the whole track, top

Announcing the new,
slimmer version of
Foreigner.

LOU GRAMM   MICK JONES
RICK WILLS   DENNIS ELLIOTT

Juke Box Hero

(Lou Gramm, Mick Jones)

This was made up of a couple of separate ideas. Lou Gramm came up with the "Take one guitar" line and part. I had the chorus and title, and as we were messing around in the studio, the two just got morphed together. Over the years this has become the closest thing to a rock anthem that I've had a hand in writing. Even now, crowds go crazy whenever we play 'Juke Box Hero.' And I'm pretty proud of the power we managed to get into the song.

RELEASED
January 1982 c/w
'I'm Gonna Win'

PRODUCED
Mick Jones,
Mutt Lange

My favourite black Gibson
Les Paul.

to bottom, and Dennis was
right on the money, absolutely
flawless. I stomped back into
the control room and said to
Mutt, quite aggressively, "Is
that what you're looking for?"
To which he could only reply,
"Well yes, I guess so."

Gradually, then, Mutt and
I began to build a mutual
respect and understanding
between us. I figured out that
he was testing me, but that he
was also incredibly diligent.
We worked a lot together on
guitar sounds and he was the
only producer I've worked with
who took the time to listen

to all the tapes on which I'd
collected riffs, solo parts, and
the snatches of beginnings
and endings for songs. In
doing so he acquired a great
understanding of what I was
doing and wanted, and he
picked out a few snippets that
later became important to the
finished album.

There were a few "firsts" for
Foreigner while making 4.
That was the first record on
which we used musicians
who were not members of
the band during sessions,
for instance. Thomas Dolby
was particularly helpful

with programming and playing the synths for
us, while Lou Reed's keyboard player Michael
Fonfara (who'd also been in Buddy Miles and
Michael Bloomfield's Electric Flag) added some
great sounds to a couple of tracks. But getting
a true Motown legend to guest on just one track
was a huge thrill for me. Jr. Walker's 'Shotgun'
and 'Roadrunner' were staple ingredients of any
decent soul jukebox, and he and his Allstars had
been one of the most successful instrumental
acts of the latter half of the 1960s. Getting him
to record with us wasn't preplanned, exactly, but
having laid down most of 'Urgent' it seemed to
Lou and me that there was space for a solo of
some kind, and we hadn't thought what, exactly,
when I noticed that Jr. Walker was playing at
the Village Vanguard on Seventh Ave. Lou's
recollection of what happened is slightly different
to mine. He recalls that we went down to see him
and asked if he'd play for us, but it had to be that
night–even though he'd finished playing at about
1 a.m. Jr. agreed, went back uptown with us and
laid down a few solos, and was done.

The one regret I have about *Foreigner 4* is that
Mutt and I didn't mix the album together. He had
to go to another job in England, so engineer Dave
Whitman and I had to finish the job. By then, we'd
already overrun by something like three months
and Hall & Oates had booked the studio after us,
and they were left hanging on for us to finish—at
one point we had to barricade the doors to stop
their roadies from breaking into the studio! After
we'd mixed 'Jukebox Hero,' I played it over the
phone to Mutt in London and to Bud Prager.
Now, Bud was not really a music connoisseur,
but like Mutt he knew how to distinguish a hit.
Almost in unison, the two of them shouted,
"Where are the background vocals?"

In the panic to finish the track, I had completely
forgotten to add the backgrounds to the chorus.

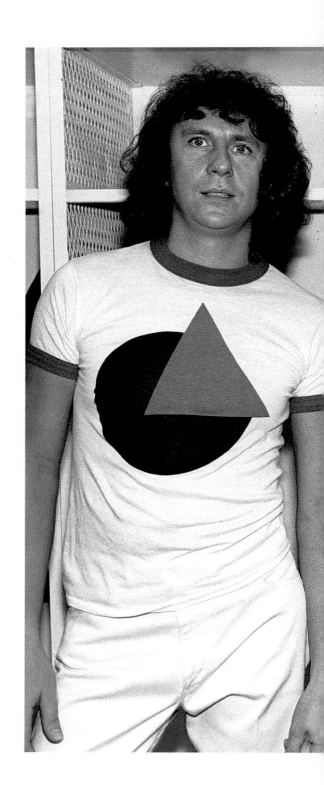

Backstage at the Rosemont,
Illinois, November 1981. (L-R)
Dennis, Lou, Rick, me.

I freaked out, but then Dave and I had been working on that one song for a week solid and were exhausted. However, we rushed back into the studio before the Hall & Oates team could get there, re-barricaded ourselves in, and Dave spliced the original vocals from the board into the master track. This was before there was any form of electronic salvation to such a problem, and we had our four hands on the boards doing all the cues. It was chaotic, panic-stricken almost, but we managed to re-do the song's four choruses in about half an hour.

Even still, it took an almost agonizing amount of time to get that album done, almost a whole year all told. Yet soon enough, that length of time wasn't considered excessive. I remember being in a club in London a couple of years later when Simon Le Bon came and sat next to me. Duran Duran had just spent an age making their *Seven and the Ragged Tiger* (1983) album and he

said to me, "We've beaten you in studio time!" It was seen as something to be proud of that you had spent a million and a half dollars on an album. Little did we all realize at the time that we would have to pay all that money back. Such were the little traps that record companies put in contracts with bands.

When I heard the final version of *Foreigner 4*, though, I knew that we had made a big album. I found writing the songs easy, they came to me almost naturally and it was at the point at which we mastered our style. The album had that mix of heaviness, soul, and ballads I'd been hoping for. But above all I think *4* strengthened our claim to be a real classic rock band. It did, though, come at a cost to me personally. The protracted recording took a lot out of me; I was there for every minute of it, and developed something of an oppressive bunker mentality while immersed in the work. After it was done, I desperately

needed a break. The effects of that intense,
drawn-out recording lasted well into the future,
and even now I have an almost psychological
problem with hanging out in recording studios.
When recording I like to get things done, and see
sunlight as often and as much as possible when
making albums.

Night Life

Instead of doing the sensible thing and take
any time off after completing the recording and
mixing of 4, I went back out on the road—the first
gig had been booked for a date just two weeks
after finishing work on the record. Arguably the
best word to describe the tour we did to promote
Foreigner 4 would be extravagant. There was
a bit too much imbibing of the cocktails of the
day, shall we say, and all too often Happy Hour

We didn't look like
hair-metal merchants,
did we?

would go on for much longer than 60 minutes (and sometimes occur at odd times of the day or night). Yet all the time that we were playing and partying, in the back of my mind there was a constant niggling question bothering me. No matter how many cocktails I downed in order to relieve myself from the boredom of being on the road when we weren't performing, I couldn't stop worrying about where we could possibly go from that point. For the next 18 months, we headlined stadiums and sold out venues all over the world. It was very tough to stay grounded in any real sense. Strangers wanted to be my friend, to "help me" with anything I wanted.

One positive side of it all, though, was that the band had started to be recognized by our peers as a serious entity. An example of that was when Jimmy Page and Robert Plant got up and performed with us at the Munich Olympiastadion in May 1982. The two of them flew out together from London for our show. That was a huge surprise to me at the time—I didn't even know they were in the building until they walked out on stage for our final encore. There and then we hastily decided to do Little Richard's 'Lucille,' but I was so in awe of them being there that I started off playing the riff to Roy Orbison's 'Pretty Woman' instead, which is similar. Jimmy yelled to me, "You're doing the wrong one!" and I corrected myself quickly enough (I hope). That was such a huge moment for me, though, when I realized that we appeared to have been accepted on that level by musicians who we could now properly regard as peers.

An opulent feast followed that show, of course, at a very exclusive restaurant in the city, the Four Seasons. At the time, every three months the Four Seasons' head chef would change the menu and the entire look of the restaurant to reflect the passing season. I remember thinking that we were walking into a fairy-tale world that night, a sort of Walt Disney version of spring-time. Mind you, lots of not-so-innocent but jolly good fun ensued over the course of our visit, in a kind of modern-day Bacchanalian feast but I'll have to leave it at that, I'm afraid...

We had a few breaks from constant gigging on that tour, and during one of them I met up with Stevie Nicks in New York in order to try and write a song together. It was titled 'The Night Gallery' after a sci-fi show that had run on American TV in the early 1970s. Stevie was just then embarking on her solo career—her first solo album *Bella Donna* came out about the same time as *4* had—and she was very much in demand, but unfortunately we couldn't quite get the song to work. It was never properly released, although there's a demo of it on YouTube somewhere, I understand. That was something I regretted, not being able to complete the song with Stevie, but it was symptomatic of how I was feeling in general at the time.

I'd simply lost focus.

By the end of the tour I was completely burnt out. But then, it had begun on September 11, 1981 and ended on August 8, 1982, during which time we played 98 shows in America alone. I felt as if

my whole life had been turned
upside-down, and so insisted
that I be allowed to take a
few months off from writing,
playing, recording—everything.
In any event, it necessarily
turned out to be a much longer
period of rest and recuperation
that was needed. It was a
question for me of simply
stopping to watch the flowers
grow for a little while. I had
been caught up in a vortex of
activity and wanted, or rather
needed, to get myself out of it
and live a more normal life. My
marriage to Felicia had fallen
apart for several reasons, and
the mad pace and scheduling
of my life had played a big part
in that.

However, in 1981 I had been
introduced to Ann Ronson by
a mutual friend, at a dinner
party. I think our mutual friend

had designs on Ann, who
had recently separated from
Laurence Ronson, the father
of her three children Mark,
Samantha and Charlotte, but
from the moment I saw her
there was no question for me
that I had to get to know her
better. I was powerless to
resist her, and the best part
of my time off from making
music in the year between
the tour ending and beginning
work again was spent with Ann
and her children.

To ensure that Foreigner
wasn't forgotten by fans while
we were off the road and not
recording, we put out our
greatest hits album, *Records*
in November 1982. It did
phenomenally well, selling
over seven million copies in
America alone.

With my third wife, Ann;
I was powerless to resist
her.

I Want to Know What Love Is

(Mick Jones)

I was in London at the time of writing this—
that was when I still kept an apartment in the
city. We'd had Thomas Dolby play keyboards
for us on *Foreigner 4* and in the studio I had
observed firsthand what he was able to do on
the Jupiter A, which back then was a cutting-
edge instrument. I went out and bought one
for myself, and got a guy from my local music
store to come round and show me how to work
it. I was just fiddling around on it one day and
came up with the opening chords to the song.

The most profound moment of creating that
track, though, was when we had the New
Jersey Mass Choir come in and put down
their part. That came about during a lunch I
was invited to by the great Jerry Wexler from
Atlantic Records. There was another guy who

RELEASED
November 1984
c/w 'Street Thunder
(*Marathon* Theme)'

PRODUCED
Mick Jones, Alex
Sadkin

joined us and he had just then bought a catalogue of gospel choirs. Originally, I had wanted to have Aretha Franklin duet with Lou on the track, but that never materialized. I was thinking out loud and this guy asked if I'd thought of using a gospel choir. To be honest, I wasn't at all sure.

I hadn't experienced a choir since singing in one at our local church when I was eight years old. But this guy insisted that it was a spiritual song and so I decided to give it a whirl.

We used a 40-voice choir, but initially couldn't get what we wanted from them. For some reason, the song wasn't quite happening. After three or four attempts, the conductor came over to me in the studio and said, "Hey man, there's something missing but we're going to see if we can find the right vibe this next time." Then he got all of us, including my mum who had happened to have dropped by that day, into a circle and asked us to say the Lord's Prayer.

After doing that, we rolled the tape again with all of us standing together. Even now, it still brings tears to my eyes when I think back to that moment. How I was surrounded by all of these soulful people and we nailed the perfect take.

That Was Yesterday

My break from music couldn't last forever though, and aware that there were now a sizable number of Foreigner fans who wanted to hear new material from us, I began to write music in 1983 for what would be the studio follow-up to the enormously successful *Foreigner 4* (which had been number 1 in America for ten weeks!).

From the outset, I didn't want to repeat the formula of the previous album though, and there was never a question of us working with Mutt Lange again. I felt that we needed a fresh perspective, so I started to collaborate with a New York engineer named Frank Filipetti. Amongst others, Frank had worked quite a lot with Carly Simon and Billy Joel (he engineered and mixed both *Piano Man* and *The Stranger* for the latter), and had recently engineered Kiss' *Lick It Up*, which had re-established them as metal superstars. I figured he had a pretty good ear. He was indeed first rate, but the trouble was that I found it difficult to get back into the swing of things. Mentally, I had allowed myself to slip off track and my wheels weren't rolling by the time we were in the Hit Factory on West 54th Street in the Hell's Kitchen district of New York. Put another way, it was as though I had blundered into a fog and couldn't find my way out.

When I at last did get some clarity back though, I decided to have Trevor Horn produce the next album with us. Trevor had just come off making the *90125* album with Yes, which had been very successful both commercially and creatively. Just as he had on that record, my hope was that he could bring in some more unusual sounding elements to fit right alongside our rock vibe. Even now I often wonder how the *Agent Provocateur* album might have turned out, had we retained Trevor to work on it, but sadly that just wasn't possible. The fact was that doing that album with Yes

As it says on the top, this is my mum's favorite photo. Can't think why.

had left him pretty much frazzled and really, he
was not in a fit state to take anything else on.
Both he and I realized as much soon after we
had started to work together and so we mutually
agreed to part ways.

Ridiculously though, when Trevor originally
agreed to work with us we had checked out of
the Hit Factory, and flown all of our gear over
to London to work with him there, and at great
cost. That made it impractical for us to move
on again, and so we were stuck fast in the old
Island Records studios, SARM West, in Notting
Hill. Out of necessity once Trevor had gone,
I started to make calls, desperate to find us
another producer. Alex Sadkin was one of the
first names to pop up. He had been a kind of
in-house producer at Island and had produced

Bob Marley's *Survival*, a bunch of Grace Jones
records, and Duran Duran's apparently eventful
Seven and the Ragged Tiger. I duly gave Alex the
job of helping me steer *Agent Provocateur*. But
that turned out to be an error on my part. Alex
had a softer approach to making records than we
were known for and I think ended up feeling a bit
impotent when in the midst of recording with us.

Certainly it reached the point in the studio where
it fell back on me to make all of the decisions. To
be honest, I wasn't at the top of my game either
though, and so a sort of vacuum developed, into
which all our ideas seemed to get lost. We never
really got going on the record, but the recording
did at least have one saving grace. At the very
beginning of the album sessions, I had played
Trevor my initial backing track for 'I Want to

Know What Love Is' and he had enthused about it, almost shouting, "That's a Number One!"

I wrote the beginning of the song in London. I was up late one night, in an apartment with Ann, who was soon to become my wife, and I walked into the bedroom at about two in the morning and said, "I've got this great idea," for which I had the first two chords of the intro and the title. She said, "So, what's it called?" I replied, "Well, it's called 'I Want to Know What Love Is.'" She looked at me and said, "What do you mean you want to know what love is? We're about to get married! Don't you know what love is?"

I guess it began life as a romantic love song, but I was listening to it one day when we were finishing the album back in New York, and I had

visions of Aretha Franklin singing on it. When we couldn't get her and it was suggested that we use a Gospel Choir instead, I called a friend of mine who owned a catalog of gospel music and gospel group recordings, and he suggested the New Jersey Mass Choir. I called them, they came in and it was an awesome two or three hours in the studio. I had never conducted a gospel choir before! They were nervous, and just before we wrapped it up with the final take, everyone got together in a circle and said the Lord's Prayer. That was *such* a moment. My mother was in the studio that day, and she, like everybody else, was in tears after the prayer. Then we rolled the tape and they nailed it the first time.

When we were close to wrapping up the album with Alex (who sadly died in a car crash in 1987),

Not exactly the piano man,
but I write songs with it.

Ahmet Ertegun paid a visit to the studio. Ahmet was very much into soul and gospel music, and I very much wanted to play him the finished track. We went and sat in a little mix room, just he and I, and I turned the lights down and rolled the tape. He started to move around in his seat, which was unusual for him. And then I'll always remember, during the second chorus I risked looking over at him and he had tears rolling down his cheeks. That I had brought the famed Ahmet Ertegun to tears with a song felt like a profound achievement for me.

Ahmet was a great character and larger-than-life figure. He was a diplomat's son and very refined in public, but a joker and nutcase in private. I would run out of adjectives if I tried to describe him any better than that, but he inspired his company and all the people who worked at Atlantic to strive for greatness. Ahmet

also presided over something of an inner circle at Atlantic, made up of the A-list whose membership included Mick Jagger, Aretha Franklin, and Ray Charles. Foreigner didn't have enough credentials to even get to meet him when we were making our first record, which was another thing that made me determined for us to make a name for ourselves. It was only after *Foreigner 4* that we at last gained entry to Ahmet's elite circle and for me it was like getting a Papal blessing.

Ahmet had a great ear and like Trevor Horn, he was proved right when 'I Want to Know What Love Is' went to Number One around the world, and so became the one song I will be remembered for long after I am dead and gone. Despite what I thought had been a troubled production process, the *Agent Provocateur* album was another massive success for us, and it does have some good stuff on it. But I have never been satisfied with it as

a whole. There were personal reasons for that as well—but they have to remain private, I'm afraid. All I will say is that I wish now that I'd had a bit more control over my own behavior at that point, and then it might have been a greater period of creativity for the band. It was such a pity, but we never quite made a proper follow-up to 4.

As it was, people started to say that we had lost our way. Although I was proud of 'I Want to Know What Love Is,' because of it we were accused of having gone soft. That, in turn, had another and more damaging knock-on effect within the band. Lou kind of jumped on that very specific criticism as a way of telling me that he didn't want to sing that style of song ever again. It wasn't as if there hadn't been any ballads on our previous records, but I think a certain coterie of advisors that he had gathered around him by then were already bumping towards doing his own thing.

I Don't Want to Live Without You

(Mick Jones)

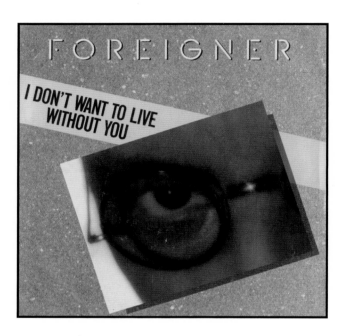

This is one of my favorite songs, and very personal to me. At the time it was written my wife Ann was eight months pregnant, and my mum was in New York visiting with us. I was sitting with mum one night, tinkering around on the piano, and came up with this chord structure. The song was pretty much written that evening. The ones that come to me so fast are usually pretty good. This, and 'Waiting for a Girl Like You,' are the two most emotionally draining songs that I've ever written. Again, it was that feeling of grabbing something from out of the air and letting it flow through me. And I still have great difficulty playing it without tearing up.

RELEASED
March 1988 c/w 'Face to Face'

PRODUCED
Mick Jones, Frank Filipetti

Reaction To Action

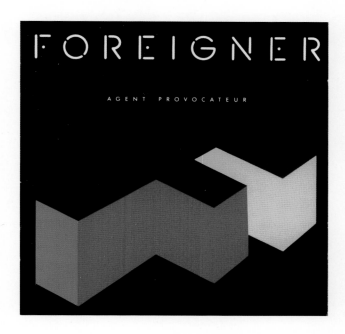

Our fifth album sold enormously well, much aided by the inclusion on it of 'I Want to Know What Love Is' (our only US and UK Number 1 hit single).

Considering just how fed up I was with studio work after making the *Foreigner 4* album, you would think the least likely thing I would do would be to go and make records with other people. However, that was precisely what happened when in 1985, I was asked to produce Van Halen's *5150*. It was a huge album for them since it was their first without singer David Lee Roth, who had quit the band and gone solo (as front men sometimes do). David isn't what you would call a great vocalist, but he is a great combination of talent and personality and he had fit Van Halen completely and as such had been a significant part of their overall sound.

I had known David's replacement, Sammy Hagar, for years. In fact, I believe it was Sammy (and

John Kalodner) who championed my cause to Eddie and Alex Van Halen as a producer for them. Both Sammy and John were fully aware of my knowledge of producing singers, which was going to be critical in this instance because it was essentially going to define the record. Indeed, I knew from the first time I heard the basic backing tracks that the band had been working on that. My main task would be to find a spot for Sammy, because they already sounded so powerful. I think that ended up being my biggest contribution to the finished record.

Ultimately *5150* turned out to be the "screw you, David Lee Roth" album. But before that had been accomplished, I had to navigate the shenanigans going on between band members, friends, and

family. The album's title is taken from the LA police code for a disturbed person on the loose, and I often felt like calling 5150 during the recording process. Eddie and Alex, in particular, were going through a rough period with each other, and things could erupt between them at any time—as it might with most brothers, perhaps. In that respect, though, the presence of their father did not help at all.

Jan Van Halen, an alcoholic former sax player, would come over to the studio and incite them to fight. He would stir up one against the other and then sit back and watch as his sons beat the shit out of each other. It seemed to give him some

sort of perverse pleasure and Eddie and Alex would really go for it too—neither of them ever hung back.

Eddie is such a talented musician that you can't help but be impressed by him. He's got a God-given gift, but like most people who are that incredibly blessed, he pays a price for it in other areas of his life. Without going into too much detail, I understood him in that sense because I had felt at times that Foreigner's success hadn't come from me. From my point of view, it was as though I was channeling something from somewhere else and that gave me power and vision. In general, I think that was how Eddie felt,

OPPOSITE: Van Halen in the
garden of Eddie Van Halen's
home and studio, 5150.
(L-R) Alex Van Halen, Mark
Anthony, Sammy Hagar,
Eddie Van Halen.
ABOVE: *5150*, the album

too. In such cases, most often you find that deep down these kinds of virtuoso people are very spiritual and just can't handle the burden of what they are capable of, nor the magnitude of regard that they're held in. It gets to be an intolerable pressure for them and they turn elsewhere for release.

The other person I had to get onside on that record was Van Halen's regular engineer, Donn Landee. Donn had worked on all their previous albums alongside producer Ted Templeman. When Ted had thrown in his lot with David and left the Van Halen camp, I think Donn had fully expected to take over from him as producer to

Eddie and Co. In Donn's mind, he had paid his dues and was part of the family, and when he realized that I was going to be involved, he got a bit weird. It mostly showed itself in his being very obviously resentful whenever I asked him to do anything. When the increasingly awkward situation with him finally boiled over one day, it did so in quite a dramatic fashion.

Van Halen's studio (which was also called 5150, by the way) was on Eddie's property and I arrived for work on the afternoon in question to find the locks had been changed. Donn was alone inside the building and had locked himself in with the master tapes. He was threatening to burn the

Me with the ace Chic guitarist and songwriter Nile Rodgers, in 1985.

place down. I don't believe his anger was entirely directed at me though—he was upset with Eddie too, I was sure. After quite a bit of talking him down, we did eventually manage to placate Donn, and after that incident there was a noticeable change in him. It was as if his blow-up had served to mellow him out and by the end of the album we had become the best of pals. We mixed the record together, and there's no doubt he is a highly gifted engineer.

It turned out to be a really good record and also one of Van Halen's most successful, being their first US Number One album. 'Why Can't This Be Love?' became the big hit single from *5150*, but the track I was most proud of was 'Dreams' (which was the second single taken from the album). I pushed Sammy way over the top on that one, so much so that when he was laying down his lead vocal, he almost passed out in the studio from hyper-ventilation. But he was very happy with the finished result, obviously.

Storm Front

Straight after wrapping up *5150* in 1986, I went on to produce Bad Company's comeback album, *Fame and Fortune*. A couple of years on from that, I oversaw another huge hit record, Billy Joel's *Storm Front*. In one way it can be said that I walked into the exact same situation on that album as I had with Van Halen because I was stepping into some very big producer shoes—this time those of Phil Ramone. Phil had produced pretty much everything that Billy had done up to that point, and was an amazing music man.

Up till then, I only knew Billy in passing at awards shows, openings or restaurants in New York where we both lived, giving each other a "Hi" here and "How you doing?" there. But I went to see him play an outdoor show at Jones Beach in New York, and we had a drink together afterwards—we were both

OPPOSITE: the cover of
Storm Front.
LEFT: Billy Joel in the
studio, not at the piano
for a change.

connoisseurs of alcohol at that time—and got on really well. Very soon after that I got the call from his management asking me to produce the album. It was a definite challenge for me, but I think Billy wanted me with him because I was a fellow songwriter. He felt he needed some support in there somewhere, and someone with an unbiased opinion.

Even so, I was nervous going in because Billy doesn't limit himself to just one style of music, he does all sorts. We got on well, each of us liked the finer things in life and I believe we had a mutual respect. But sometimes it's hard to have to tell another songwriter certain things. For example, one day Billy came to me with a song he had written called 'Jolene.' And I'm sure it wasn't a conscious thing, but the fact was that he had kind of unknowingly ripped off the Dolly Parton song of the same name. So I had to pluck up the courage and tell him that he had taken rather a lot from Dolly.

When I'd finished telling him, Billy gave me a really offended look, but he kind of shrugged, said, "Uh, OK," and walked off. He went and sat down in another part of the studio building, summoned his assistants and told them to bring him all of the *Time Life* almanacs dating back from the present to the year of his birth (1949). He read through all the *Time Life* mags and wrote down the prominent happenings in each year since he had been born, and then put them together as a lyric. Doing that allowed him to transform 'Jolene' into 'We Didn't Start the Fire.' Then he walked back into the studio and said to me, "Check this out," but in a way that quite apparently was meant to suggest, "Screw you." A thank-you would really have been more appropriate, but I knew five seconds into the re-arranged song that it was a hit.

At the time of making *Storm Front* Billy was going through the beginnings of the break-up of his marriage to Christine Brinkley. Towards

the end of the sessions, I listened to the album one night by myself and thought we had two big, strong single tracks with 'We Didn't Start the Fire' and 'The Downeaster 'Alexa'' (the name of his only daughter). But I felt we were missing one more. I wanted three hits, so I pestered and nagged Billy about it, and to the point where he told me forcibly, "No more! Christie wants me to stop and I'm going to lose everything if I don't." Eventually, of course, he stopped making records altogether, although that was after he and she had divorced. Still, that's the only regret I have about that record—it needed just the one more song, another hit single. Of course, in 1993 Garth Brooks had a much, much bigger hit with 'Shameless' than Billy's version had been; if only I'd thought of taking Billy's Dolly Parton inspiration and making it a country song...

Years later I bumped into Phil Ramone in New York and I didn't really know what kind of reaction I would get from him, but he said to me,

"Mick, I have to tell you something. When I heard that Billy was going to work with somebody else I was really angry—until I heard the album. I couldn't have thought of anyone better than you to produce it, so hats off." That was a very nice confirmation. All I did was to help Billy enhance his songs by working with him on the arrangements and the overall sound of his band. I did also get into his vocal phrasing a little bit with him, but he's such a great singer that he didn't really need that kind of support.

I did expect, or at least hope, that Billy and I might work together again in the future, but his life took a different course. I was given to understand that his whole entourage pressed him to use me on his next album, *River of Dreams*, which proved to be his last pop record (to date, anyway). But again, he probably didn't necessarily want to go back to the same approach and sound, and I can appreciate why that would be the case.

Bad Love

(Eric Clapton, Mick Jones)

This was written while I was making *Storm Front* with Billy Joel. At the same time, Russ Titelman, who I had gotten to know quite well, was producing Eric's *Journeyman* album. Russ called me up and asked if I'd be interested in going over to the studio and hanging out with Eric to see if we could come up with something together. I was definitely very nervous to be sitting around playing guitars with Eric Clapton, but it was funny how that song ended up coming about. I started to play the main riff, which I have always thought sounded a bit like Jeff Wayne's *War of the Worlds* theme. Eric got quite animated and told me, "That's exactly what I need, because people are always fucking asking me to do another 'Layla!'" Eric subsequently came up with the chorus, but it was ironic that it should be me who ended up referencing his most beloved song and not him.

RELEASED
March 1990 c/w
'Before You Accuse
Me'

PRODUCED
Russ Titelman

Sharing the Rock and Roll Hall of Fame stage with Keith Richards in 1989, the year they were inducted into the museum.

The closest analogy I can think of for what a record producer does would be the role of a director in the movies. You develop the album, like a script, and then have the same responsibility of preparing all the details that go around it before you embark upon making it. For me as a producer, the lead vocalist is my main actor and I think I specialize in getting the best possible performance out of singers. After all, doing that was how I came up with both Sylvie and Johnny, when I worked in Paris.

There are lots of people who claim to be producers, but they don't do anything beyond the technical aspects of recording. For me, you have to go further than that to properly produce. You have to gain the trust and respect of the singer and other musicians. You have to have the ability to ride the vibe in the studio on any given day. If you come in to work and everybody's feeling worn down or just shitty in general, then it's up to you to play the psychologist and pick the mood up. I learned a lot from working with Van Halen and

Billy Joel especially, artists who were their own entities. As a producer I was really a visitor to somebody else's world, and as such I got to see everything—good and bad, the whole gamut of another artist's creative process. That was very instructive, but I don't now have any real burning desire to produce another band or performer. Obviously, a lot of the facets of recording have changed in the last 20 years or so, and not always for the better as far as I can see. And like I said, these days I value daylight too much.

Inside Information

There are certain situations that cannot be resolved by even the most accomplished, or diplomatic, producer. The plain fact is that the identity of a band is usually created by its singer, and that can't help but be the case, because the singer is the focal point and his or her voice has to get into people's psyche. Undeniably it makes things difficult when a singer decides to go off and make a solo album. It's usually a shock for the rest of the band for a start, and nine times out of ten it never really works.

From the moment that Lou Gramm went and made his first solo record, *Ready or Not* in 1986 with Bruce Turgon (who co-wrote all the songs and played bass on the album) the die was cast for him and Foreigner. Lou's album sounded to me very much like a Foreigner record. And that wasn't helpful since we were set on releasing our next album in the same year, 1987. I couldn't help but take it personally, and felt a bit offended at hearing my style being played by other people on his album, which came out in January of 1987.

Lou and I could be the best of friends on occasion, but I always had a feeling that he didn't entirely trust me, and that hurt a lot. I believe I did so much for him by putting him in Foreigner in the first place, and essentially making him a star. I also helped him to develop as a singer, and introduced him to a different kind of phrasing

than he'd been used to until he joined the band. It was that which gave him and Foreigner such a strong identity.

I admit that at times I'd push Lou hard with his voice, but then I knew that he had the capacity to handle it. By the *Agent Provocateur* record, though, I guess he felt I was asking him to go too high. However, making them sing at the very the top of their range is prominently marked in the record producer's instruction book for keeping lead singers in check. I knew too that *Ready or Not* would not be a one-off. Ultimately, I was convinced that it was going to break up the band and in doing so, risked throwing away everything that we had created over the previous ten years. I also knew that being out on his own would be very tough for Lou, because by that time he had become a bit of a reclusive personality and at least with Foreigner he had me to share publicity duties, and we'd do interviews together whether on TV, radio, or for music papers.

Earlier in the year we'd begun rehearsals for the new album, but suspended them while Lou went on tour to promote his solo album. When that finished and we started again, Lou would drive down to New York from where he lived out in the country near his hometown of Rochester, and be in and out of the studio as quickly as he could. I think he would have preferred it if he could have

OPPOSITE: Pure bliss,
with my daughter
Annabelle Dexter-Jones
BELOW: The *Inside
Information* cover.

done his parts by phone. He didn't play a bigger part than that throughout the sessions, which was not what we were used to, at all. I produced the album with Frank Filipetti, but not Lou, who used to help out on that side of things. He was completely divorced from me on *Inside Information* and his input was missed in every respect—it ended up being our least successful album to that point.

Inevitably, Lou left the band not long afterwards. He went on and made a second solo album (*Long Hard Look*, in 1989) and then formed a new band, Shadow King (who released one album *Shadow King*, in 1991), but didn't get anything like the acclaim that he'd had with Foreigner. To be honest, he wasn't completely to blame for the split. Towards the end of that era of the band, I suppose that it had gotten to be me exclusively running the show. Over the years, Lou had grown increasingly frustrated that he wasn't involved more in the production process, and in hindsight he probably could have been. Back then, though, I was convinced that my way was the right way. Which is probably why, although I didn't have much of a thought to do a solo album, the fact that Lou had released two made me think that I'd give it a shot. It was great fun to make, but I could have done with giving it more concentration to be stronger in certain areas, focus on a few different parts of the recording. But it was great working with Billy Joel and Carly Simon on my record, rather than the other way around. Being able to say that they formed a part of my backing singers along with Ian Lloyd and Ian Hunter felt unreal, somehow.

A still from the video graphics that supplied the cover image for my solo album in 1989.

There's a great sax solo on one of the tracks on *Mick Jones*, called 'Wright Tonight,' played by Lenny Pickett, who'd been a part of Tower of Power in the 1970s, and he was then, and still is, the excellent bandleader from *Saturday Night Live*. Some of the songs on my solo record I thought were good, but the album didn't get any airplay, so few people heard it—which meant few people bought it, of course.

But then, there was so much else going on which sounded very different and that the radio stations were playing. Tastes were changing and I hadn't perhaps fully caught onto how they were changing, nor given enough thought about how I and Foreigner might adapt to the changing times.

Unusual Heat

Of course, given that Lou had left Foreigner, our next album could perhaps try to be something different to *Inside Information*. Naturally, finding a replacement for Lou was anything but easy. I eventually got to hear of Johnny Edwards when I was sent a CD of material that producer Keith Olsen (who'd worked with me on the Bad Company album *Fame and Fortune* in 1986) was working on with his band, Wild Horses. Straight off I was taken with his voice which has more of a blues feel to it than Lou's. Johnny was also very versatile and a real showman on stage, which again was different to Lou. Jann Wenner, the publisher of *Rolling Stone*, flew me out to LA on his private jet to meet with Johnny and then bring him back to New York. That was the first experience Johnny had of Foreigner.

During Johnny's time with the band, we had a lot of fun together. Actually, he was a bit of a

loner, but he had a good sense of humor and didn't take himself too seriously. He was very conscientious, too. It certainly made a pleasant change from the difficult, dour atmosphere that had settled on us over the preceding couple of years. As such, we were full of optimism when we started work on what would become the *Unusual Heat* album with Terry Thomas. Before we began Terry was reluctant to work with Johnny, simply because he wasn't Lou, but once we started working together, and I had both of them writing songs with me, things began to work out. I always thought it was important, from the early days of the band, to work with the singer and first of all have him feel part of the process, and realize that it's him who's singing the songs, so he has to capture the feeling or the direction of the song. It was a gesture to welcome Johnny into the band and I knew that he had written songs, so it wasn't just me saying, "Oh, he writes a little." He had the experience of writing and it was a fun experience working with

him and he fully deserved the credits that he has on the album.

I had a very good feeling about it, for sure, and initially that seemed as if it was going to be borne out. The finished record was very much in the classic Foreigner style and it got a great reaction when it was first released in 1991. Despite what Lou seemed to think, I had certainly never made any conscious decision to go "soft" or to become a keyboard-oriented band. It was just a phase we were going through. If you look at a lot of the big bands over the years, they've experimented and I never wanted to feel stagnant with the music from Foreigner. I think, by and large, we were able to do that and on *Unusual Heat* we were, I thought, back to what we do best. I remember the first time that I was in LA after it came out. I was driving down Sunset Boulevard with the radio cranked and on came the first single from the album, 'Lowdown and Dirty.' I still love that feeling when you've just

MICK JONES   RICK WILLS   JOHNNY EDWARDS   DENNIS ELLIOTT

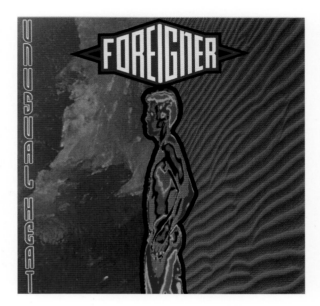

done a record and you hear it being played on the radio for the first time. It never fails to blow my mind. That particular afternoon, I turned the volume up even higher and slammed down the accelerator. Right then I thought we were going to be unstoppable.

Unfortunately for us though, the whole music scene in America was undergoing a massive sea change by 1991. First of all, you'd had Mötley Crüe and all those glam-metal bands, and that had started to turn off a lot of our audience from rock music. That was when people began to make the shift towards country music as a replacement for classic rock because I think they saw country as having the same authenticity to it, which the hair-metal bands perhaps lacked. Then Guns N' Roses happened, and after that the whole grunge thing. Nirvana, of course, released *Nevermind* in 1991 and, at a stroke, we were very definitely not the taste of the day anymore.

Unusual Heat didn't get any real traction on radio and sort of fizzled out. It wasn't a complete failure, but appeared that way when compared to our back catalogue.

When attempting to promote the album we were asked to make a live radio appearance in Frankfurt, Germany and were offered the Atlantic company jet to get there and back in a day. Perhaps because things hadn't been going too well, a little friction had built up between us in the band, but for some reason I agreed to this trip, but it all became a little surreal. We took off from New Orleans with this world-famous chef traveling with us, who then cooked us a meal while on board the plane. The whole thing felt to me as if we were being transported without really wanting to be. During the flight Rick and I got into a tussle over a game of chess or something. We had great affection for one another but this felt as if things were getting to be out of kilter; there was a lot of tension—were we doing the right thing, being on a corporate jet, flying to Frankfurt and back?, I kept wondering. At some point as we came in to land the realization dawned on me that I was headed

down a tough road, and taking the band with me and I took exception at something Rick had done or said, and we had a kind of fight, which continued as we disembarked, with the others trying to keep us apart. It was comical but at the same time tragic, somehow. It was also a sign of exactly how disjointed Foreigner had become and throughout the rest of the 1990s we slipped off the charts and came to be regarded by many as a kind of nostalgia act. That was a view which endured for the next few years.

It was perhaps inevitable that Lou should come back into the fold the following year, especially since he had also struggled with Shadow King. He was kind of happy making our next record, 1994's *Mr Moonlight*. He had a new girlfriend, and we made the album in Woodstock near to where he lived in upstate New York. In turn, I was made very happy to be able to work with one of my childhood heroes on *Mr Moonlight*.

It was odd, but before Duane Eddy arrived at the studio, I felt nervous, which I didn't remember feeling about working with anyone else. He was lovely, though. I showed him what I wanted him to do and he plugged into his tiny amplifier that was already set up for him, and nailed the solo on 'Until the End of Time,' first time!

It was a genuine pleasure to induct Duane into the Rock & Roll Hall of Fame in 1994 (almost as much of a pleasure as having accepted Eddie Cochran's induction in 1987), and to be able to say that I worked with him. However, that was a dark period in general for Foreigner. Rick and Dennis had ended up leaving the band after *Unusual Heat* along with bass player Bruce Turgon. Even though Lou and I co-produced *Mr Moonlight*, it didn't ultimately fare any better than its immediate predecessor had done.

BELOW: (L-R) Bruce Turgon, Lou Gramm, Mr and Mrs Jeff Jacobs, my mum, Alexander Dexter-Jones, me, Ann Dexter-Jones.
OPPOSITE: The *Mr. Moonlight* album failed to reverse the band's fortunes.

The final dates with Lou
singing, 2002.

Until the End of Time

In 1997, I was producing an album for an Australian singer, Tina Arena, and she was recording a version of 'I Want to Know What Love Is' for it. I wanted to have Lou come down and sing on it so I rang him and asked, and he duly turned up at the studio and appeared to be in super shape, with not an ounce of fat on his body, and his singing was great. There was one small problem with his session because he had a slight memory lapse over the lyrics, but I didn't think too much of it at the time. However, it wasn't more than a few weeks later that he was diagnosed with suffering from a brain tumor.

Fortunately, Lou's doctors were able to operate on him before the tumor became unstoppable, but he had a long, slow recovery. The medication that he was prescribed caused him to balloon in weight and he was in no condition to work. But even though both Bruce Turgon and I tried our best to dissuade him, Lou insisted on going back out on the road with us the following year. We tried to support him as much as we could, and on a brotherly level we were obviously concerned for his well-being. Eventually, it got to the point where Lou simply could not perform live. And in the end, very sadly, his last shows with Foreigner were on our 25th anniversary tour of 2002.

The band simply did not feel right to me at that juncture, either. Bruce Turgon had been Lou's principal co-writer on his solo albums and in Shadow King, so having him in Foreigner made for a strange situation. He and I never got to be comfortable around each other. So, when Lou left us again, I thought that it was probably time for me to pack it in as well. I would have done so, too, had it not been for a phone call I received from Jason Bonham.

Kelly Hansen was so mild-
mannered offstage that
I doubted he'd be
a good frontman:
how wrong I was.

Jason rang to find out what I was up to and why we weren't out on the road. When I told him that I had to all intents retired, he said: "You're crazy! There are so many people out there who still want to hear those songs." Jason doesn't pull his punches, and he was very convincing and his energy and sheer enthusiasm were a big boost. Subsequently, Jason and I met up in New York and had a little jam together, and that was essentially the start of the next phase of Foreigner. Jason brought Jeff Pilson with him to play bass and I included two guys who by then had been part of the touring group for several years, Jeff Jacobs on keyboards and multi-instrumentalist Thom Gimbel. We found our new singer pretty much hidden under a rock out in the San Fernando Valley.

We held open auditions for the job, and they were a sort of karaoke test with each candidate being asked to sing along to four instrumental tracks. Kelly Hansen came in looking very studious; he had on reading glasses and was carrying a jotter pad in which he wrote copious notes. Obviously, he was very nervous. I had heard his previous band Hurricane and liked the sound of his voice on record, but he had by then basically given up performing. He was doing little bits of production here and there, and recording the odd radio jingle, but nothing more. Like the rest of us, his career had suffered from the grunge factor. When he sang along to the tracks, he was quite clearly miles ahead of anyone else we had auditioned. He was in.

The one thing I wasn't sure about with Kelly was his appearance. He just didn't carry himself like a lead singer I thought; he was so mild-mannered. But that changed from the very first gig we did with him at a club in New Mexico. It was a warm-up for a tour and Kelly came out of the dressing room that night in tight pants, torn T-shirt, looking every inch the rock star, and he blew the roof off the place. In a way, he was the guy I had always been hoping to find—a frontman who was also a showman. Lou was a great singer, but he'd never been a big mover on stage. Kelly's been an integral part of Foreigner ever since.

To begin with we had to go back out and play the clubs; we had fallen that far out of the mainstream. That was tough, and it felt like we were paying our dues yet again, but we hung in there and slowly worked our way back to playing bigger and more prestigious venues. We did so even though we made just the one new record since 1997, and that was *Can't Slow Down* in 2009. It was an odd album to make in a way, because it was recorded in part on the road, sometimes in hotel rooms, and in one instance out on the street so that you could hear pedestrians walking by. There are some good songs on there, I think, but perhaps unsurprisingly, the only way that we stood a chance of getting anything new played on radio was to come out with a big ballad.

Can't Slow Down

As a whole, *Can't Slow Down* could have been a little harder-edged. But I did at least have the pleasure of working with my stepson, Mark Ronson on it (he produced Fool for You Anyway). That was fun, because I'm pleased to say that Mark takes a real retro approach to making records. He collects vintage equipment and as such is able to get that authentic '60s, '70s soul sound. He was obviously surrounded by music growing up and I gave him complete access to my record collection, which is primarily where he picked up many of his influences. He loved classic rock at the time and still does. Living in New York, he also immersed himself in hip-hop and dance culture as he grew up. But Mark was always willing to listen and eager to learn. He

would ask me how the guys played a song or about a guitar part here or there, so I did kind of semi-tutor him. He's a very talented, very bright guy and capable of putting his mind to anything. Having worked on records with Lady Gaga, Bruno Mars, and Amy Winehouse he really hit his stride, I think.

Family life has been very important to me—and it's been eventful, too. I have four children and three stepchildren and I am equally devoted to and proud of each of them. They, in turn, seem proud of what I have accomplished in my career. Five of the seven have a Foreigner-related tattoo somewhere on their bodies. As Mark once said to me: "You cannot possibly think that what you've done hasn't affected this family." Ann and I were divorced in 2007, but we re-married and so managed our own kind of happy ending.

The Flame Still Burns

(Chris Difford, Marti Frederiksen, Mick Jones)

This was originally written for a British film, *Still Crazy*. I got a call from the director, Brian Gibson because the two of us had worked together on the video for 'I Want to Know What Love Is' and had become friends. Brian told me that he was desperate for my help and needed seven songs for the soundtrack to his film. "And by the end of next week," he added. At the time, I was working with another good friend of mine, Marti Frederiksen and somehow he and I managed to write five or six new songs in that time. The title was already earmarked for the final song in the movie, though, and Chris Difford of Squeeze had written a set of lyrics. Jeff Lynne had also written a version of the song using Chris' words. Our version was chosen over Jeff's and to this day he still thinks that I stole the title from him. I think we've overcome that now, but it was a sore point for me because I've always been very careful about plagiarism. Anyway, it ended up winning us an Ivor Novello Award. Foreigner cut a new version of it in 2016 which seems to me to have a timeless quality.

RELEASED
November 2016 c/w
'Feels Like the First
Time'

PRODUCED
Mick Jones, Jeff
Pilson

Through everything, my family have been my rock and
never more so than when I got sick in 2011 and 2012.
In truth, it began as a complete nervous breakdown,
which hit me out of nowhere. At the time, I was taking
anti-depressants under a doctor's supervision and
had just had my medication changed. I don't know
what happened, but it knocked me sideways and took
three months of rehab for me to feel better. In fact, I'm
still on anti-depressants. It's something that I use to
stabilize myself and thankfully I haven't had any more
anxiety attacks since then.

When I went to get a check-up I discovered that I had
severe blockages in some of the arteries to my heart
and had to have an aortic bypass. A friend who worked
in the emergency room at a hospital down in Miami,
where I also have a home, made all the arrangements
for the procedure. That took me more time to recover
from, and it was a rough couple of years.

I suppose going through those kinds of experiences
does prompt you to look back and re-evaluate your
life. I'm pleased that I've stuck in there with the band

I'm lucky enough to have
a home in Florida, where
I can get away from
everything.

The lineup that persuaded me that there was life left yet in Foreigner. (L-R, back) Thom Gimbel, Paul Mirkovich, Kelly Hansen, (L-R, front) Jeff Pilson, me, Jason Bonham.

and that we have soldiered on. Today, writing songs is difficult though, especially with us having been around for so long. I simply wouldn't know how to change Foreigner's musical direction or become more "modern." However, people tell me that my music is going to be around for a long time and outlive me. I find that a bit melodramatic, but I guess there is a chance that it just might.

A huge validation of my career came when Lou and I were inducted (by Billy Joel) into the Songwriters Hall of Fame in 2013. That helped to eradicate a lot of the self-doubts I'd had about myself over the years. Lou and I performed a couple of songs together using acoustic guitars that night in New York, and there was no question for me that we wouldn't, since we were both nominated and I guess he felt the same. We got together to rehearse a couple of days beforehand and it was a little weird, but not in a negative sense. We hugged and said how much this meant to us—and there was some mutual pride looking back at what we had both achieved.

On the night, we performed 'I Want to Know What Love Is' with a full choir, and apparently it was one of the highlights of the evening. There were some big names in the room that night, too, a lot of very venerable people of whom I had long been in awe. I had a bit of an emotional breakdown on stage, but it was a magical experience. The last thing Lou and I said to each other when we parted that night was, "We'll have to get together again." I've no intention of having him re-join the band, I think he knows that, but we do have some musical ideas that we might be able to work on and put on a future album as bonus tracks or something. I'm not against that at all.

The following year, I was also able to close the circle on my relationship with Johnny Hallyday. He was doing a short tour of the States at the time and called me and asked if I would get up with him at the Beacon Theatre in New York. That night, we performed a song together that Tommy Brown and I had written for him, 'Oh Ma Jolie Sarah' and Johnny was still able to sing it and all the other songs in the keys in which they were written, which I thought incredible. He looked great, too.

Earlier in the day, the two of us went out for a bite to eat. Over lunch, Johnny told me that he was now finally able to forgive me for leaving his band all those years ago. I didn't realize at the time quite how much it had meant to him, but he said to me: "Man, for all of these years that has been one of the most heart-breaking things in my life." In turn, I was able to tell him how much he had taught me about performing and I thanked him. I guess all along he was the big brother I never had.

OPPOSITE: (L-R): Bruce Watson, Me, Kelly Hansen, Jeff Pilson and Thom Gimbel playing an acoustic set at the T.J. Martell 40th Anniversary NY Gala at Cipriani Wall Street in New York City, 2015. Those acoustic tours are great fun.

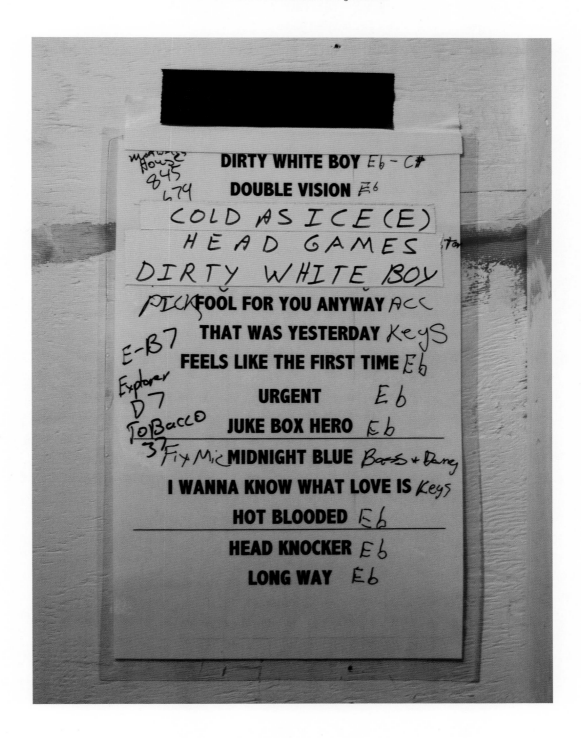

LEFT: As long as I'm having fun, I'll keep on doing it. FOLLOWING PAGES: The Foreigner 40th Anniversary lineup (L-R) Chris Frazier, Thom Gimbel, Kelly Hansen, me, Jeff Pilson, Michael Bluestein, Bruce Watson

I don't like to dwell too much in the past, though. Foreigner's 40th anniversary tour, which kicked off in July 2017, was something of a celebration of the band's longevity, and represents something of an achievement, I think. It was very gratifying to be able to play a couple of rather prestigious venues, Carnegie Hall in New York and—at last!—The Royal Albert Hall in London.

Almost 60 years after witnessing Buddy Holly on my family's black-and-white television set and deciding that was what I wanted to do, I still can't think of anything else I would rather be doing with myself. There's no grand plan for the future, just the intention to take it one day at a time. I want to continue to watch my kids make their way through their lives and careers, and be just as good a dad to them as I can possibly

be. I read quite a lot, enjoy watching movies, and I'm quite happy and perfectly contented. I certainly don't want to end up playing golf down in Miami, riding around on a cart, wearing black pleated trousers and smoking a cigar—in fact, I can't think of anything worse.

No, I've led a pretty full life, and up till now I've survived it, so I mean to keep on keeping on, and am nothing but grateful.

Spellbinder

(Lou Gramm, Mick Jones)
[June 1978]

If I had to pick out just one song of mine, it would be this, the closing track from the *Double Vision* album. I love the mood that we were able to capture on it; I thought it was kind of sophisticated sounding. It was a different sort of song for the band and one where we went out on a wing a bit. I still love it.

Discography

band / artist | title | released as | year | Mick's role - ● musician/producer, ● musical supervisor, ● writer/arranger (France: 1964-72)

Hector Et Les Médiators, Il Faut Saisir Sa Chance (From the *Cherchez L'idole* aoundtrack), 1964 ●

Sylvie Vartan, Il N'a Rien Retrouve, e.p., 1964 ●●

Sylvie Vartan, Et Pourtant Je Reste Là, e.p., 1965 ●

Cliff Richard & The Shadows , The Time In Between, single, 1965 ●

Noel Deschamps, Je N'Ai À T'Offrir Que Mon Amour, e.p., 1965 ●

Sylvie Vartan, Quand Tu Es Là, e.p., 1965 ●

Francoise Hardy, Tu Peux Bien, e.p., 1965 ●

Sylvie Vartan, Dans Tes Bras, e.p., 1965 ●

Thierry Vincent, Je Ne Peux Pas L'Oublier, e.p., 1965 ●

Johnny Hallyday w/ The Blackburds, Noir C'Est Noir, e.p., 1966 ●●

Johnny Hallyday, Si J'Etais Un Charpentier, e.p., 1966 ●●

Johnny Young & Kompany, *Young Johnny*, album, 1966 ●●

Johnny Hallyday, Je L'Aime, e.p., 1966 ●●

Dick Rivers, Mr. Pitiful, e.p., 1966 ●

Elsa Leroy, Mademoiselle Âge Tendre 1965 Chante, e.p., 1966 ●

Ronnie Bird, N'écoute Pas Ton Coeur, single, 1966 ●●

Johnny Hallyday, A Tout Casser, e.p., 1967 ●●

Ronnie Bird, La Surprise, e.p., 1967 ●

Johnny Hallyday, Amour D'Ete, single, 1967 ●●

Sylvie Vartan, *Sylvie Vartan*, album, 1967 ●

Johnny Hallyday, Entre Mes Mains, e.p., 1967 ●●

State Of Micky & Tommy, Frisco Bay, single, 1967 ●

State Of Micky & Tommy, With Love From 1 To 5, single, 1967 ●

State Of Micky & Tommy, Frisco Bay, e.p., 1967 ●

State Of Micky & Tommy, With Love From, e.p., 1967 ●

Johnny Hallyday, *Johnny*, album, 1967 ●●

Johnny Hallyday, *Olympia '67*, album, 1967 ●●●

Johnny Hallyday, San Francisco, e.p., 1967 ●●●

Johnny Hallyday, *Jeune Homme*, album, 1967 ●●●

Johnny Hallyday, Cours Plus Vite Charlie, single, 1968 ●●

Johnny Hallyday, L'Histoire De Bonnie And Clyde, e.p., 1968 ●●

Ronnie Bird, Le Pivert, single, 1968 ●●

Johnny Hallyday, *Que Je T' Aime*, album, 1969 ●●

Johnny Hallyday, Ceux Que L'Amour A Blessés, single, 1969 ●●

Johnny Hallyday, Rivière... Ouvre Ton Lit, single, 1969 ●●

Sylvie Vartan, J'ai Caché Le Soleil, single, 1969 ●

Ronnie Bird, Sad Soul, single, 1969 ●

Johnny Hallyday, Que Je T'aime, e.p., 1969 ●●

Sylvie Vartan, C'est Un Jour À Rester Couché, e.p., 1969 ●●

Johnny Hallyday, *Johnny Hallyday*, album, 1969 ●●●

Francoise Hardy, *Alone*, album, 1970 ●

Francoise Hardy, Dame Souris Trotte, single, 1970 ●

Johnny Hallyday, Deux Amis Pour Un Amour, single, 1970 ●●

Isabelle De Valvert, La Di Dou Dam, single, 1970 ●

Micky Jones & Tommy Brown, If I Could Be Sure (from the film *Tumac Humac*), single, 1970 ●

Micky Jones & Tommy Brown, L'ours et la Poupée (from the film *L'ours et la Poupée*), e.p., 1970 ●

Francoise Hardy, Dame Souris Trotte / Point, single, 1970 ●

Francoise Hardy, Soleil / Je Fais Des Puzzles, single, 1970 ●

Francoise Hardy, *Soleil*, album, 1970 ●

Johnny Hallyday, *Vie*, album, 1970 ●●●

Martin Circus, *En Direct Du Rock 'N Roll Circus*, album, 1970 ●

Johnny Hallyday, Fils De Personne, single, 1971 ●●

Johnny Hallyday, *Flagrant Délit*, album, 1971 ●

Thomas F. Browne, *Wednesday's Child*, album, 1971 ●●

Peter Frampton, All I Want To Be (Is By Your Side), album track, 1972 ●

Johnny Hallyday, *Country - Folk - Rock*, album, 1972 ●

Francoise Hardy, *If You Listen*, album, 1972 ●

Gary Wright & Wonderwheel, *Ring Of Changes*, album, 1972 (Released 2016) ●

Gary Wright, *Benjamin - The Original, Soundtrack Of Willy Bogner's Motion Picture*, album, 1972 ●

Thomas F. Browne, Gentle Sarah, single, 1972 ●

Francoise Hardy, *Francoise Hardy*, album, 1972 ●

Spooky Tooth, *You Broke My Heart So...I Busted Your Jaw*, album, 1973 ●

Spooky Tooth, *Witness*, album, 1973 ●

Jerry Lee Lewis, Memphis, and Rock 'n' Roll Medley, album tracks, 1973 ●

Spooky Tooth, The Mirror / Hell Or High Water, single, 1974 ●

Spooky Tooth, *The Mirror*, album, 1974 ●●

Johnny Hallyday, *Je T'aime, Je T'aime, Je T'aime*, album, 1974 ●

George Harrison, Ding Dong, Ding Dong, album track, 1974 ●

Tim Rose, *Tim Rose*, album, 1972 ●

Johnny Hallyday, Hallyday Story 22 - 1971 / Flagrant Délit, single, 1974 ●

Spooky Tooth, Fantasy/Satisfier, single, 1974 ●

Spooky Tooth, Two Time Love, single, 1974 ●

The Leslie West Band, *The Leslie West Band*, album, 1975 ●

Carol Grimes, Number One In My Heart, single, 1975 ●

Carol Grimes, I Betcha Didn't Know That, single, 1975 ●

Ian Lloyd, *Ian Lloyd*, album, 1976 ●

Foreigner, *Foreigner*, album, 1977 ●●

Foreigner, Cold As Ice, single, 1977 ●●

Foreigner, Feels Like The First Time, single, 1977 ●●

Foreigner, Long, Long Way From Home, single, 1977 ●●

Foreigner, Hot Blooded, single, 1978 ●●

Foreigner, Lonely Children, single, 1978 ●●

Foreigner, *Double Vision*, album, 1978 ●●

Foreigner, Blue Morning, Blue Day, single, 1978 ●●

Foreigner, Women, single, 1979 ●●

Foreigner, Head Games, single, 1979 ●●

Foreigner, *Head Games*, album, 1979 ●●

Foreigner, Dirty White Boy, single, 1979 ●

Foreigner, Love On The Telephone, single, 1979 ●●

Foreigner, Dirty White Boy, single, 1979 ●

Ian Lloyd, *3WC**, album, 1980 ●●

Foreigner, Waiting For A Girl Like You, single, 1981 ●

Foreigner, *Four*, album, 1981 ●

Foreigner, Urgent, single, 1981 ●●

Foreigner, Juke Box Hero, single, 1981 ●

Foreigner, Luanne, single, 1981 ●●

Foreigner, Break It Up, single, 1981 ●●

Foreigner, Waiting For A Girl Like You, single, 1981 ●

Foreigner, I Want To Know What Love Is, single, 1984 ●●

Foreigner, Reaction To Action, single, 1984 ●●

Foreigner, Down On Love, single, 1984 ●●

Foreigner, *Agent Provocateur*, album, 1984 ●●

Foreigner, That Was Yesterday, single, 1984 ●●

Foreigner, Growing Up The Hard Way, single, 1984 ●●

Foreigner, Down On Love, single, 1984 ●●

Jean Beauvoir, Rockin' In The Street, album track, 1986 ●

Bad Company, This Love, single, 1986 ●

Van Halen, Dreams, single, 1986 ●

Van Halen, Why Can't This Be Love, single, 1986 ●

Van Halen, *5150*, album, 1986 ●

Van Halen, Best Of Both Worlds, single, 1986 ●

Bad Company, *Fame And Fortune*, album, 1986 ●

Van Halen, Love Walks In, single, 1986 ●

Van Halen, 5150, promo single, 1986 ●

Foreigner, *Inside Information*, album, 1987 ●●

Van Halen, Good Enough (from *Spaceballs* Soundtrack), album track, 1987 ●

Foreigner, Say You Will, single, 1987 ●●

Foreigner, I Don't Want To Live Without You, single, 1987 ●●

Ben E. King, Halfway To Paradise, single, 1987 ●

Ben E. King, Save The Last Dance For Me, single, 1987 ●

Foreigner, Heart Turns To Stone, single, 1987 ●●

Flesh And Blood, *Dead, White & Blue*, album, 1987 ●

Billy Joel, *Storm Front*, album, 1989 ●●

Ian Lloyd, *Goosebumps*, album, 1989 ●

Mick Jones, Everything That Comes Around, single, 1989 ●●

Mick Jones, *Mick Jones*, album, 1989 ●●

Billy Joel, We Didn't Start The Fire, single, 1989 ●

Billy Joel, I Go To Extremes, single, 1989 ●

Billy Joel, Leningrad, single, 1989 ●

Billy Joel, And So It Goes, single, 1990 ●

Billy Joel, The Downeaster "Alexa", single, 1990 ●

Billy Joel, That's Not Her Style, single, 1990 ●

Foreigner, I'll Fight For You, single, 1991 ●●

Foreigner, *Unusual Heat*, album, 1991 ●●

Foreigner, Low Down And Dirty, single, 1991 ●●

Foreigner, With Heaven On Our Side, single, 1992 ●●

Foreigner, *Mr. Moonlight*, album, 1994 ●●

Foreigner, White Lie, single, 1994 ●●

Foreigner, Until The End Of Time, single, 1995 ●●

Foreigner, Rain, single, 1995 ●●

Tina Arena, *In Deep*, album, 1997 ●●

Tina Arena, Burn, single, 1997 ●●

Tina Arena, I Want To Know What Love Is, single, 1997 ●●

The Scorpions, 10 Light Years Away, album track, 1999 ●

Brian Howe, Don't Ask Me Why, album track, 2003 ●

Foreigner, *Live in '05*, Album, 2006 ●

Foreigner, *Alive And Rockin'*, album, 2007 ●

Foreigner, *Can't Slow Down*, album, 2009 ●●

Foreigner, *Acoustique*, Album, 2011 ●

Foreigner, *Feels Like The First Time*, album, 2011 ●●

Marianne Faithful, *Give My Love To London*, album track, 2014 ●

Foreigner, *An Acoustic Evening With*, album, 2014 ●●

Foreigner, The Flame Still Burns, single, 2016 ●●

Index

Roll of honour

The publishers gratefully acknowledge the contribution of everyone listed below, whose generous support has helped bring this project to fruition.

Ken Adams

Dr. Michelle Aheron

Allison Allinson

David Areen

Mary Armand

Pip Arnold

Jacques Arsenault

Juan & Antonio Auli, father & son from Columbia

Jeffrey "Hammer" Bachman

Michael A Bailowich

Xander Bakker

Stephany Barkofsky

Craig Baxter

Richard Belanger

Mary & Rick Bohne

Teddy Bollinger

Maria Bruch

Baden Butler

Ethan Campbell

David Cassick Jr.

Vinnie Castaldo

Clara Cerniglia

Nick Cerro

Barbara Champ

Mark P Coleman

Bob Colon

Jim Connors

Alan & Saeko Crawford

John Czaja

Danymoonchild

Chris Davis

Jorge Martin Delgado

Jeff DeLuca

Randy Dieter

Christine Dobies

Jackie & Al Dolynchuk

Shannon Dominick

Paul Drennan

Christian DUVAL

Roy Edginton

Eric Edmondston

Cerene Whalen Fassio

Gregg Feiertag

Nick Ferrantella

David Finkelstein

Tony Finocchietti

Sandra Fisher

Roger Flaming

Sven Olaf Förtsch

Janet Fournier

Dana Frey

Alan Frizzell

Joanne Fucci

Dave Garrard

Rob Gauder

J. Gavin Brown

The Gedemondan

Fritz Geller

Jonathan Grace

Martha Bush Graf

Jeff Graham

Nigel Griffiths

Phillip Hackney

Boaz Halachmi

Joseph Hankin

Lucas Hannon

Zachary Kipp Hansen

Tom & Vera Harder

Ron Havener

Kevin & Jacqueline Herrington

Sherry Herrington & Tim Herrington

Carmen Herzog

Lynn Heydenreich

Michael Hillman

Ralf Hirse

Julie Holle

Daniela Hommes-Wochau

Randall W Hood

Gina Hyams

Karen I. Silins

Bobby Ireland

Tony Isabella

Javier Izurieta

Shawna Jackson

David James

Ralph Jenkins

Andrew Johnstone

Eric Jourdan

Jane K

Nancy Keeton

Eunice Kelly

John H. Kerr

Paul A. Klempa

Melanie Kneidl

Kelly Koper

Joyce Krawczyk

Kim Kucner

Brittney N. Kurth

Cara Lambert

Mike Lambert

Peter Langelaan

Peter Langford

Ofie Lattman

Rosemarie Leipply

Bill Leonard

Joost Leonard

Louis Levin

David Liverman

Mike Lowe

Babs Marks

Martial

Adrian Martin

Fabian Martinez

Terry McCall

Roy McClurg

Brian Perry & Debbie McDaniel

Tanya "Blonde Bombshell" McGowan

Calum John McGregor

Kyle "Sarge" McKone

EuGeNe McMaNuS

Meryl McMorran

Mike Mettler

Dave Miedema

Andy Mills

Cathey Moore

Joseph Natishan

Merced Ness

Brian Nickerson

Mark Niemeyer

Mick O'Connor

Larry Oakes

Mike Owen

Elaine & Kaleo Palakiko

Leslie A Palleria

Bill Peel

Chrissy Peel

Joe & Alison Perry

Jill Philpott

David Pinder

Wesley Plimmer

James Polito

Wendy Porter

Elizabeth Posey

Mark Pridmore

Mark R. Walsh

Nicole Rambo

Stephanie Rambo

Danny Reynish

Ralph Richter

Mario Rieger

Raymond M. Riethmeier

Josee Riopel

Luis Rivas

Brenda K Robinson

Carol Robinson

Todd Rorick

Keko Ruiz

Jean Ryan

Wendy S.

Didier Saltron

Tracy Sellers

Craig Shoosmith

Joe Siegler

Spence

Richard Spray

Michael Staertow

Eric Steiner

Christian Stumpp

Mark Swindell

Tricia Tabar

Julie Takata

Kristina Telge

Debra Thomas

Paul Thomas

Tapani Tikkanen

Danielle Todd

The Fabulous Jennifer Tyler

Jennifer Ufnowski

C. David Wagner Jr.

Terry Welty

Ken Wheeler

Ricky Willette

Richard Wise

Bill Yonak

David R. Young

May C. Young

Picture credits

Page 2-3: Len DeLessio/Getty Images, 5: Mick Jones collection, 6: Mick Jones collection, 7: Mick Jones collection, 8: Mick Jones collection, 9: Mick Jones collection, 11: Mick Jones collection, 12: Metronome/Getty Images, 13: Michael Ochs Archives, 14: David Redfern/Redferns, 17: Mick Jones collection, 18: Courtesy Colin Green, 19: Hulton Deutsch/Corbis Historical, 21: Mick Jones collection, 22: Mark and Colleen Hayward/Redferns, 23: Associated Press, 24: Mick Jones collection, 25: Associated Press, 26: Mark and Colleen Hayward/Redferns, 28: Associated Press, 29: Associated Press, 30: Pathé EMI Records, 31: Keystone-France, 32: Phototheque Rancurel, 35: LE TELLIER Philippe/Paris Match Archive, 36: Keystone-France/Gamma-Keystone, 39: Roger Viollet, 40: Phototheque Rancurel, 43: Popperfoto, 44: Mick Jones collection, 45: RCA Victor, 48: Mick Jones collection, 49: GAB Archive/Redferns, 51: Phototheque Rancurel, 53: Lipnitzki/Roger Viollet, 55: Reporters Associes/Gamma-Rapho, 56: Philips Records, 57: Philips Records, 59: Reporters Associes/Gamma-Rapho, 60-61: Keystone-France/Gamma-Keystone, 63: Jean Pierre Bonnotte/Gamma-Rapho, 64: Phototheque Rancurel, 67: Phototheque Rancurel, 68: Mercury Records, Philips Records, 69: Mercury Records, 70-71: Mick Jones collection, 72: RDA/Hulton Archive, 74: Graham Wiltshire/Redferns, 75: Keystone-France/Gamma-Keystone, 76: Neil Leifer/Sports Illustrated/Getty Images, 78-79: Keystone-France/Gamma-Keystone, 80: Mick Jones collection, 83: Pictorial Press/Alamy, 84: Mick Jones collection, 87: Pictorial Press/Alamy, 88: GAB Archive/Redferns, 89: Shinko Music/Hulton Archive, 90: Fox Photos/Hulton Archive, 91: ABC Photo Archives/ABC , 92-93: Brian Cooke/Redferns, 95: Jorgen Angel/Redferns, 96: Terry O'Neill/Iconic Images, 98: Alain Le Garsmeur/Corbis Historical, 99: New York Post Archives/NYP Holdings Inc, 100: Island Records, 101: Michael Putland/Hulton Archive, 103: John G White/Denver Post, 104: Goodear Records, 105: Len DeLessio/Getty Images, 106: Robert Altman/Michael Ochs Archives, 107: Phantom Records, 108: Len DeLessio/Getty Images, 109: Michael Ochs Archives, 110: Waring Abbott/Michael Ochs Archives, 112: Waring Abbott/Michael Ochs Archives, 113: Waring Abbott/Michael Ochs Archives, 115: Paul Natkin/Getty Images, 116: Len DeLessio/Getty Images, 117: Atlantic Records, 118: Michael Putland/Hulton Archive, 121: Len DeLessio/Getty Images, 122: Hulton Archive, 125: Mick Jones collection, 126: Paul Natkin/WireImage, 127: Mick Jones collection, 128: Atlantic Records, 129: Ebet Roberts/Redferns, 130: Atlantic Records, 131: Atlantic Records, Mick Jones Collection, 132: Atlantic Records, 133: Mick Jones collection/Cash Box, 135: Mick Jones collection, 136: Waring Abbott/Michael Ochs Archives, 137: Atlantic Records, 138-139: Paul Natkin/Getty Images, 140: Atlantic Records, 142: Waring Abbott/Michael Ochs Archives, 145: Gus Stewart/Redferns, 146: Atlantic Records, 149: Granamour Weems Collection/Alamy, 150: Atlantic Records, 151: Waring Abbott/Michael Ochs Archives, 153: Paul Natkin/Getty Images, 154: Atlantic Records, 155: Ron Galella/WireImage, 156: Ebet Roberts/Redferns, 159: Ann Clifford/The LIFE Picture Collection/Getty Images, 160: Atlantic Records, 163: Mick Jones collection, 164: Mick Jones collection, 165: Ron Galella/WireImage, 166: Michael Putland/Hulton Archive, 168: Atlantic Records, 169: Atlantic Records, 170: Ann Summa/Hulton Archive, 171: Warner Bros. Records, 172: Ron Galella/WireImage, 174: The LIFE Picture Collection/Getty Images, 175: Sony Music, 176: WEA International, 177: Mick Jones collection, 179: Ann Clifford/The LIFE Picture Collection/Getty Images, 180: Mick Jones collection, 181: Atlantic Records, 183: Mick Jones collection, 184: Michael Ochs Archives, 185: Atlantic Records, 186: Arista, 187: Mick Jones collection, 188: R. Diamond/WireImage, 190: Harry Herd/Redferns, 192: e•a•r music, 193: Rhino Records, 194: Mick Jones collection, 195: Christie Goodwin/Redferns, 196: Mike Coppola/Getty Images Entertainment, 197: Jane Phillimore, 198: Bill Bernstein, 199: Paul Natkin/Getty Images, 200-201: Bill Bernstein

Disclaimer